LAVENDER ROAD TO SUCCESS

LAVENDER ROAD TO SUCCESS

The **Career Guide** for the **Gay** **Community**

Kirk Snyder

TEN SPEED PRESS
Berkeley | Toronto

1🖉

Ten Speed Press
PO Box 7123
Berkeley, California 94707
www.tenspeed.com

Distributed in Australia by Simon & Schuster Australia,
in Canada by Ten Speed Press Canada, in New Zealand by
Southern Publishers Group, in South Africa by Real Books,
and in the United Kingdom and Europe by Airlift Book
Company.

Cover and text design by Catherine Jacobes

Library of Congress Cataloging-in-Publication Data
Snyder, Kirk.
    Lavender road to success : the career guide for the gay
community /
Kirk Snyder.
    p. cm.
    ISBN 1-58008-496-6
1. Gays—Employment. 2. Homosexuality in the
workplace. 3. Career
development. I. Title.
HD6285 .S693 2003
650.1'086'6—dc21   2003011973

Printed in the United States
First printing, 2003

1 2 3 4 5 6 7 8 9 10 — 07 06 05 04 03

This book is dedicated to
the members of the USC Lambda Alumni Association.
Through their generosity of time, honesty, and spirit,
they have made an unparalleled contribution
to advancing and improving the world of work
for the gay community.

DEDICATION

CONTENTS

PREFACE

THROUGHOUT THE BOOK I HAVE USED the words *gay* and *lavender* to mean anyone who self-identifies as lesbian, gay, bisexual, or transgender. The appropriate distinction is made in certain instances to accurately reflect specific research facts or case studies.

THE UNIVERSITY OF SOUTHERN CALIFORNIA has played a major role in my life for more than twenty years. This book would not have been possible without the renowned Trojan family, and specifically the USC Lambda Alumni Association. I am humbled by the overwhelmingly positive response I have enjoyed from the association's leadership, and of course all of the members who made my research and this book possible. Foremost, I'd like to thank Dr. Mary Andres, President of the USC Lambda Alumni Association at the time I began my research. I will forever appreciate your collegial support and friendship.

Also at the top of my thank-you list at USC is Eileen Kohan. You believed in the importance of this project from the beginning and made it possible for me to pursue my own dreams in the world of work. You encouraged me throughout this journey and kept me laughing. Thank you always for your continued support. To my dear friend Dr. Elizabeth Davenport, I will forever appreciate all that you've done to effect positive change at the university and in the world. You have inspired me more than you'll ever know. Special thanks to Dr. Cynthia Cherrey for her expert advice and guidance on navigating the waters of writing a book. I thoroughly appreciate all of your encouragement and support along the way. Last, but certainly not least, at the university, I'd like to thank Dr. Michael L. Jackson for creating a workplace environment in the division of student affairs that is diverse, welcoming, and affirming for all people. Your compassionate leadership sets a high standard in the field of higher education.

Beyond the ivy at USC, my first thank-you goes to my agent, Felicia Eth. From the first time we spoke on the phone, I knew we would have a successful partnership. Thank you for believing in this project and always being my truthful and loyal advocate. To all of the talented people at Ten Speed Press, beginning with Julie Bennett, my extraordinary editor, a heartfelt thank-you. I will always appreciate your amazing eye,

ACKNOWLEDGMENTS

encouragement, and guidance. It was a pleasure working with you on this book. Many thanks also to Kirsty Melville, who believed in the importance of this book and its estimable audience. Thank you for giving my work a welcoming and inclusive home.

Success of any kind is meant to be shared with those you love most, and this book is certainly no exception. Being able to formally thank the people who enrich my life every day is a privilege. First and foremost, my love and thanks go to my parents. You've given me the freedom to be myself, and you will never know how much your love and support have enriched my life. You've always been in my corner, and the emotional security you have provided in my life is immeasurable. To my partner Kirwan, thank you for believing in the value of my dreams and cheering me on to the finish line! You have been patient and giving, for which I will always be grateful. Your insight and talent as a trusted sounding board have guided me throughout this entire process. To my best friend, Christine, having you back in my life has been a great gift. Thank you for all of your encouragement and support. Twenty years after we first met at USC, your love and friendship are represented in my past, present, and future. When it comes to family, it's often said that we can't pick our relatives. However, there is one relative in particular that I am lucky to call family. To my cousin Yvonne, thank you for always being my number one advocate. I am extremely fortunate to have all of you in my life.

YOU CAN START ENJOYING THE FREEDOM to be gay and successful today. Based on your own unique identity, you can achieve your professional dreams without limits in the real world of work.

Who you are as a human being is unquestionably the most important professional asset you possess. Integrating your sexual orientation into your career empowers you to achieve a higher level of success because you're able to utilize the total strength of your individuality. Just as you wouldn't overlook any type of noteworthy accomplishment or ability that provides value in the working world, you shouldn't overlook or underestimate any part of your overall identity.

As a researcher and educator in the field of career development at the University of Southern California, I can state without hesitation that for far too long, the gay community has been underrated as a collective force in the workplace. In many ways, we've been a hidden population. As a gay man whose own career is focused on the study of work in contemporary society, I've found a tremendous need for developing specific knowledge along with a practical approach for creating and attaining professional success. Out of that need grew one of the largest research projects ever conducted on the subject of career development within the gay community.

Beginning in the fall of 2000, the initial phase of my research was a direct and comprehensive survey of the membership of the University of Southern California's Lambda Alumni Association. This research provided more than three hundred highly detailed responses chronicling past and present career experiences within the gay community. The survey first identified each person's individual demographics, including age, sex, gender identification, sexual orientation, geographic location, and educational background. Quantitative questions exploring workplace realities addressed experiences of on-the-job homophobia, salary history, domestic partnership benefits, gay employee resource groups, and length of time spent with each organization. Additional qualitative questions focused on the degree each person has been in or out of the closet in their professional lives as well as the perceived positive or negative impact that being gay has had on their careers. Finally, questions related to the workplace environment addressed the professional impact of gay-friendly bosses and colleagues, employers' recognition of the transgender community, and the number of upper management positions held by those who are gay and out of the closet.

A week after I mailed out the survey, I went to the post office to see if anyone had responded. I would have been content with a few responses but was elated to find nearly fifty completed surveys waiting in my mailbox. Within a month, I had more than two hundred responses; soon after that I had more than three hundred.

As I read through the surveys—and the personal letters that accompanied so many of them—it became clear that this volume of information could not be fully represented in an article or journal. As the project grew, I began to consider how I might take all of these amazing experiences and give them even greater meaning. By the time the interviews began, my research project had turned into a book project.

The second phase of my research pulled back the covers on the percentages and numbers and examined the rich professional histories of those people who participated. Over a two-and-a-half-year period, more than one hundred twenty people from the initial survey, ranging in age from twenty-three to eighty, volunteered to share their information about their lives and careers through in-depth interviews. Excerpts from forty-eight of these interviews appear throughout the book, primarily under the heading "Talking about . . . ," and bring real-life significance to each researched fact.

You'll meet many people who believed that they weren't worthy of having a successful career because of their sexual orientation. Through their highly personal accounts of working under adverse circumstances, you'll gain insight into how to avoid these difficulties in your own professional life. You'll meet other people who did believe in their right to be gay and successful and find out how they've forged rewarding careers based on their own unique identities. Through their experiences, you will learn how to develop a road map for making career decisions that empowers you to achieve your professional dreams. Wherever you may be in your own career, and whether you're in or out of the closet at work, there's invaluable insight to be gained. Learning about the experiences of other gay professionals who have followed different paths will enhance your own road to success.

This book is organized in three distinct sections, beginning with "Developing Your Foundation for Success." Understanding the vital role your identity plays in your road to success will provide you with criteria to enhance your career. Original exercises will help you identify specific tools for developing and sustaining your highest level of professional success. For example, in section two, "Creating Your Lavender Success," you will find exercises designed to help you pinpoint real-life career "ingredients" that will move you forward in your career. Because many of the exercises call on you to record your answers and experiences, you might want to dedicate a new notebook for this purpose. Also included in section two is a specialized career planning framework developed as a result of my research. The Seven Points of Success framework allows you to organize all of the elements that go into creating a successful career into a dynamic guide to be used throughout your professional life. The final section of the book, "Achieving Your Dreams as Yourself," pulls together all of the concepts, real-life facts, and proven wisdom of others in a way that empowers you to take action on your terms, based on the value of your own identity.

When it comes to planning your career, it's vital to follow a process that allows you to accumulate strength as you move forward. By building on concepts that are presented in this book in a step-by-step fashion, you'll acquire the ability to move forward in a way that's both reasonable and achievable. All three sections are designed to work together to facilitate a beginning-to-end process. My goal for you is to realize your lavender road to success by first establishing your foundation, developing a personalized road map, and, finally, creating an action-oriented strategy to achieve your professional dreams.

As you begin to discover everything that I've discovered as a result of working on this amazing and rewarding project, never doubt for a second that the immeasurable value of who you are as a unique human being has everything to do with your ability to succeed. In order to become successful, you must believe you can be successful. And that's where your road begins.

DEVELOPING YOUR FOUNDATION FOR SUCCESS

Lavender Success Begins with You

EVERYONE READING THIS BOOK is capable of achieving success. How do I know this about you since we've never met? Because you already own the two basic ingredients that go into any successful career. First, you have a unique identity, which is the very foundation of your ability to succeed. Second, you have dreams. Even if you haven't allowed yourself to dream for a very long time, or have simply been too busy to even think about making professional changes, your dreams exist.

The process of transforming your dreams into reality includes the discovery of all the benefits your unique identity brings to the professional table. In fact, a career based on who you are in the world—and not who you think you should be, or who society wants you to be—will allow you to articulate, nurture, and pursue your dreams in the bright light of day. And if you doubt for a second that it's possible, keep reading. You'll soon start believing in your own lavender road to success.

Putting Yourself in the Picture

What do you envision when you picture success? Maybe it's money, or maybe it's what money can buy. How about a beachfront estate with a spectacular ocean view? Perhaps a luxurious month-long vacation during which you're attended to night and day is more to your liking. Or maybe your picture of success is a backyard hammock and a cottage in the country, miles away from the honking horns of a big city. Sound good so far?

Sure it does, except that in all of these scenarios, the power source fueling these successes is never mentioned.

Now wait a minute. You're probably thinking, "No, I definitely picture myself in that beachfront estate." But I'd like you to think in a different way as you begin your road to success. A multimillion-dollar home in Malibu or Maui cannot become "successful," and a first-class vacation isn't capable of "achieving." It's only you that can become successful, and you have the right, the ability, and the freedom to fully pursue that success as yourself. In other words, when you picture success, the first thing I want you to envision is you.

In order to realize your professional dreams, you must begin to recognize that you are the source of your achievement.

Granting Yourself the Authority to Achieve

Your road to success is yours and yours alone. It's unique, exceptional, and real. We all know that no one actually succeeds in life totally on their own, nor would it be any fun to always be a solo act. But believing that you deserve success does begin and end with you. Granting yourself the right to achieve your dreams is something you can do on your own, no matter where you are in your career. Later in the book we'll address this issue in greater detail, but for now, all I ask is that you begin to open yourself up to the reality that you already have all you need to begin creating a career without limits.

TALKING ABOUT . . . DESERVING SUCCESS

Mark is a thirty-six-year-old gay man who has worked hard to believe that he deserves to be successful. Before moving to Los Angeles at the age of thirty-three, he spent more than ten years with a real estate development company in central California. Mark told me that within the company, anti-gay jokes and homophobic remarks were a daily occurrence. "For the most part, the real estate development field is an all-white, very homophobic industry that doesn't allow anyone who's gay to survive. To make matters worse, along with two business partners, my grandfather started the company fifty years ago, so in many ways it's a family business. Working in that environment made me feel like I was trapped twenty-four hours a day."

Along with his original survey, Mark sent a very personal and detailed letter describing how he had remained in a destructive setting because he didn't feel worthy of pursuing success based on his own identity. He described how he had been married at an early age in order to prevent rumors about his sexual orientation from circulating around his hometown. "I was married at twenty-five, divorced at twenty-nine, and those four years gave me an alibi. And not just to my family and the other people at work, but to myself." Mark also told me that it wasn't until after the death of his last surviving parent that he was able to start believing in his right to have professional dreams of his own, separate from those of his family.

It doesn't matter if you're one year or fifty years into your professional life, you can begin to achieve success from this point forward.

A few weeks after I received Mark's letter, we arranged to meet for an in-depth interview at the university. After a brief tour of campus to show him a few of the new buildings and green spaces at his alma mater, we walked to the local coffeehouse across the street. In the same way that his letter was extremely honest and open, he was remarkably candid in person. Mark told me that for most of his adult life he didn't feel like he deserved to have choices in his career. Growing up in a fundamentalist family that he describes as "completely controlling and dysfunctional," he developed an approach to life that was "rooted in fear." He always thought of his professional life in terms of limits and boundaries because he was conditioned to think that being gay was a "shameful secret."

When Mark graduated from college, his first instinct was to look for a job in Los Angeles. His family, however, convinced him to return home and work for their real estate development company. "My father was a lot bolder than my mother and came right out and asked me if I wanted to stay in L.A. to be with 'the queers.' I think one of the reasons I decided to go back was just to prove him wrong."

Sitting in the coffeehouse, Mark picked up his drink and looked around at the students studying for their winter finals. "My greatest regret has always been returning to a life after college that was destructive, just because I bought into all the bullshit that said gay people didn't deserve to be successful." One year to the day after his father's funeral, he sold his share of the company to his brother and cousin and accepted a job as the marketing manager for a large Southern California builder. "It's amazing how feeling free to be yourself can start to change your life." He said,

When you surround yourself with people who value your unique identity, you actively dispel the lies designed to prevent you from achieving success.

"When I moved to back to L.A. after almost eleven years, I felt like I had a chance to start my life over even though I wasn't out of the closet. But once I got settled and started to meet new people, my life began to change. Sometimes, almost to my amazement, I realized that everyone wasn't like my family or the people in my hometown. And that realization gave me the hope and encouragement I needed to break away from my past."

After being in Los Angeles for a little more than a year, Mark found himself engaged in life in a brand-new way. "One day I was walking down the street and I found myself actually looking straight ahead instead of down at the sidewalk. It was a totally new perspective for me." At that point, Mark began to focus on his future. In his pursuit of success without limits, Mark made the decision to enroll in graduate school and go after his MBA. At the time of our first interview, he was more than halfway there. "I have incredible friends who are encouraging me and supporting my dreams. In my old life, I wouldn't have had the energy to go back to school, let alone succeed."

A year later, I met Mark for a follow-up interview. He was about to complete his MBA and had accepted an offer to work as a marketing consultant with a Los Angeles firm that specializes in new business expansion. Mark originally learned about the firm from a friend's partner. "I knew I'd have the opportunity to be out of the closet without any hassles, because there are other gay people at the firm. It isn't even an issue, which will be a new experience for me. Even in L.A., the real estate development field is still suffering from a lot of homophobia, and I refuse to be trapped again by other people's prejudice."

The dramatic contrast between Mark's life today and the life he was leading a few years earlier is directly connected to his granting himself the authority to define his own value. "I didn't have the courage to stand up for what was right in the face of my family and, to a greater extent, in a culture that's steeped in prejudice. I also bought into the belief that I was less of a person and actually immoral because of the fundamentalist propaganda I heard growing up. Believe me, my parents weren't righteous, they were bullies. And they were bigots." With remarkable candor, Mark revealed a great deal about the social dynamics of his childhood. "Looking back on it now, my parents believed that going to church gave them the right to act superior. I even remember, as a little kid, coming home in the car after church and hearing my father make racist comments about people walking down the street. I was raised with the inaccurate belief that you had to be straight and white in order to be successful." Taking a deep breath, he paused for a moment. "That's why it took me so long to even feel like I was good enough to succeed as myself. Sometimes you can't escape hate until it dies."

Overcoming the negative influences of society, possibly including those of your own family, doesn't require that you wait for events that are beyond your control to occur. There's no need to delay taking action that will move you forward toward your professional dreams.

Creating a Professional Life without Limits

When I began my research, I knew that my goal wasn't simply to report facts, but to interpret the facts in a way that would provide real-life career solutions. Creating a level playing field, on which you have the opportunity to achieve and succeed as yourself, is the main objective of your lavender road to success. Recognizing and appreciating that who you are has value to an employer who embraces diversity as a positive aspect of their business can be discovered by examining the successful paths of gay people everywhere. Whether your goal is to work for a small start-up or a Fortune 500 company, placing yourself in a job that connects you to your dreams is possible, plausible, and attainable.

Evaluating an Organization's Culture

The culture of any organization is a by-product of its founders, managers, employees, and geographic location. In section two, we'll identify the primary causes of homophobia in the workplace and map out strategies to defeat them on your road to success. But for now, simply recognize that regardless of field or industry, the majority of workplace environments that limit opportunities for the gay community to succeed exhibit one or more of the following five characteristics:

- There is an overall lack of respectful behavior toward all minority populations within the organization.
- The organization's clients are largely homophobic.
- The region where the organization is located lacks diversity.
- The majority of employees or clients have fundamentalist religious values.
- The organization's leaders have not been exposed to the value of diversity.

The thing that each of these characteristics shares is ignorance and fear. Why is this important to your career? As a member of the gay community, you must reject the influences of gay bigotry in order to create a professional future without limits. Your dreams are equal in value to everyone else's dreams, and you deserve the same chance to succeed.

Believing in Your Future

When you believe you're worthy of success, your dreams become achievable. One of the most significant subjects I studied in my research was the correlation between whether someone was in or out of the closet at work and the value placed on one's professional future. Of all the survey respondents, 47 percent said they were currently out of the closet to everyone at their respective workplaces, and 42 percent reported they were not. During the in-depth interviews, I asked questions that got to the heart of how people in both groups felt about their career goals, their plans for the future, and the value they felt they provided to an employer. For those people who are out of the closet in workplaces that welcome gay employees there was a stronger overall belief in their personal right to succeed. They also took more active ownership for their professional futures, meaning that they were planning or taking some type of action that would presumably move their careers forward.

Dr. Mary Andres, clinical psychologist at the University of Southern California, shared with me her expert opinion about the link between being out of the closet and being fully engaged in your career. "The idea of a professional life without limits speaks to the notion of self-efficacy. If a person is closeted, the fear or threat of discovery will disempower and critically limit one's capacity to succeed. Keeping secrets carries a price. When someone is in the closet, he or she carries an increased sense of being a fraud, or an 'Impostor Syndrome.' When we do not integrate the multiple aspects of identity, there is a greater tension. Our emotional resources are split. Our lives are not separate chapters, but one mosaic. The healthiest manifestation of our identity is embracing and seeing the complementary benefits of all parts together."

For some members of our community, believing that they have the right to be gay and successful has never been in question. For others, that belief has been acquired over time, often in the face of tremendous adversity. Still others struggle to believe that they deserve to realize their professional dreams because they haven't always felt valuable as individuals.

TALKING ABOUT . . . PROFESSIONAL DREAMS

I met Julie in her senior year of college when she came to my office for interview advice. She asked me what she should do to "make a company like me." Completely focused on one Wall Street investment firm, she told me that although she'd like to be out of the closet at work, she didn't want to hurt her chances of being hired in case the firm preferred straight employees. The first thing I asked her was why she thought it was more important to be who a potential employer might want her to be, rather than who she really is—a talented young gay woman with a great deal to offer the world of work. Her response spoke right to the heart of how she felt about her own professional value. She said, "I don't want them to think less of me because I'm gay and not get the job. So if I know exactly what kind of people they're looking for, I can give them what they want."

Throughout the semester, Julie dropped by my office several times to let me know where she was in her highly targeted job search. No matter what I said, she remained determined to go to work for a company that, in spite of having sexual orientation as part of its equal opportunity statement, in reality was known to be homophobic. Even after I put her in touch with several contacts in New York who confirmed the antigay culture of the firm based on firsthand experience, she remained determined to become part of the company. Ultimately, she felt that working for such a prestigious firm was going to be her ticket to a successful career.

After two months of interviews Julie received the offer she'd been waiting for and accepted the position on Wall Street. When I saw her at graduation, all decked out in her cap and gown, she said, "Don't worry about me. I'm just securing my success." I knew it wouldn't do any good, but once more I reminded her that she was the source of her success, not a company that won't allow its employees to be themselves. She smiled, gave me a hug, and disappeared into the throng of other proud graduates and their families.

A year and a half later, midway through my research, I received a survey and letter from someone very familiar in New York City. Julie was in the process of looking for a new job and applying for graduate school at NYU, and she noted that her personal life was in complete disarray. When I called her to check in and find out more about her experiences on Wall Street, I heard a maturity in her voice that wasn't there the last time we spoke. She said, "There's no better place to get humbled than New York City. It forces you to face yourself because it's all about brutal honesty!" She shared with me her new perspective, so different from her feelings on graduation day. "Going into this whole experience, I was convinced that this company was the absolute career maker of all time. But I had it assbackward, and now I hate going to work." I asked her what it was about her job that she hated most. "It just feels like I'm squished when I walk in the door." She paused, "It's just a really horrible fit. I want out—out of the closet, out of the company, and out of the field."

A few months later, I called to see how things were progressing in her job search and was very pleased to hear that she had been accepted into NYU's School of Public Service. She had also just started a new job as a financial consultant for a well-known corporate philanthropic foundation. I asked her what advice she'd give to someone considering going to work within an environment that doesn't recognize the strength of their unique identity. She didn't have to think about her reply. "It's not worth it to force yourself into someone else's shoes all day long. If you have to change into another person before you go to work, it's not a place where you should invest your time."

Taking Ownership of Your Career

If you were to think of your career as a movie, there's one important casting fact to remember: you need to play the leading role in your professional life because it simply doesn't exist without you! When you take ownership of your career you realize you have the authority to direct the course of your career as well as define its meaning: you're the one who gets to decide what your career is all about. Deciding how you want your career to enhance your life allows you to place yourself on the road to success and empowers you to move forward.

There are four primary factors that influence the way you feel about your career and professional future. Each factor plays a significant role in creating a sustained belief that your work is meaningful and important.

- The degree to which you view your sexual orientation as a positive attribute of your overall professional value

- The degree to which you view your work as being connected to your personal values and beliefs

- The degree to which you view your work as contributing to positive and rewarding personal relationships

- The degree to which you view your work as adding to the quality of life of others

Making career choices requires thinking about what *is* important to you, rather than what you think *should be* important based on the opinions of other people. For example, if financial wealth is extremely important to you, your career should provide you with meaning relative to the importance of financial wealth. If altruism is of the utmost importance to you, then your career should reflect this value. By defining what's important to you in your professional life, you're giving yourself real criteria for creating a career that's authentic, achievable, and meaningful.

• • •

Learning how to turn your dreams into an achievable reality calls you to fully engage the strength and value of your own unique identity. This may be an entirely new way for you to think about your career and professional future, but when you place primary importance on who you are as a human being and align yourself with an organization that recognizes your tremendous value, you empower yourself to achieve your highest possible level of success. A fulfilling and successful career is always based on what matters most—you.

It Pays to Be Out
of the Closet

As a college student in the 1980s, I never imagined myself returning to my alma mater as an educator and researcher. My strong connection with the university was brought full circle the first semester I taught Theories of Career Development. I was assigned the same classroom where I'd attended a creative writing class years earlier, giving me an extreme case of déjà vu. But one major difference between then and now, aside from the fact that I'm almost twenty years older, is that I'm now out of the closet both personally and professionally. The freedom to be myself at work adds meaning to my life that I didn't have as a closeted student. And, because I am out within a welcoming environment, I am able to fully utilize the strength of my own identity, expanding the course curriculum to include issues of gender, ethnicity, and sexual orientation. Along with my colleagues I redesigned the course and added a classroom symposium that addressed the importance of employee diversity in the world of work. Professionals representing organizations such as Charles Schwab & Company, Disney, Dreamworks, Ford, and TRW shared with students why a diverse workforce is critical to remaining at the top of their industries. Many executives attending the event were themselves members of diverse communities, including the gay community.

Victor Playa, a senior executive with a major health-care company, was a presenter at the first symposium and has since become a good friend. Victor immigrated to the United States nearly thirty years ago at the age of seventeen, in search of both personal and professional freedom. Victor has since achieved an amazing level of career success while remaining steadfast in his support of workplace equality. A firm believer in placing yourself with an organization where the "fit" allows you to achieve, he has incorporated this approach into his own career.

Everyone involved with the first symposium was anxious for it to turn out well. We wanted it to be a shining example of why it's important to continue developing career programs that address workplace diversity—at our own university and beyond. When it was time for Victor to speak, he began by asking a student in the front row, "What size suit do you wear?" When the student answered, he quickly asked another young man the same question. Needless to say, in a roomful of college-age men and women for whom body image is a very big issue, I was starting to get a bit concerned about his line of questioning! Just then, he turned the tables on himself. Getting out of his seat and standing in front of the packed room, Victor asked, "Can everyone see my suit?" Much to everyone's amusement, he jokingly modeled his clothes as if parading down an imaginary catwalk. As the laughter subsided, he said, "It's very wide and very short—just like me!" With a smile, he referred to the two students he had spoken to a few moments earlier. "Now, can you imagine either of these two guys, who are young and tall and in great shape, wearing my suit?" With great purpose he zeroed in on his message. "The reason my suit is just right for me is because it was fitted to my needs as a unique individual. Why in the world would you think about shopping for a job that isn't tailor-made just for you? After all, you 'wear' your job at least five days a week, and it should always fit the truthfulness of your heart, mind, and spirit." The room was completely silent. As he returned to his seat on the panel, the students broke into applause. Now, I'm going to ask you a question. Whose suit are you wearing? Is it fitted to your own unique identity or someone else's heart, mind, and spirit?

Finding the right professional fit, where you have the freedom to work and achieve as yourself, requires you to address the role sexual orientation plays in your career. Why is your sexual orientation so important? Because when you embrace the entirety of who you are in the world and recognize that the freedom to be yourself increases your ability to succeed, you secure your potential for absolute achievement.

Recognizing the Benefits of Being Out

Tim Gill, the founder and former chairman of Quark, Inc., and now the chairman of the Gill Foundation, shared with me his wisdom on the subject of being out in the workplace. As one of the country's most successful entrepreneurs, he's also been a major employer. "I've seen people, even gay people that have worked for me, spend too much of their emotional energy trying not to be found out. In fact, it was annoying to me when I found a gay employee who was trying to hide, because sexual orientation is not something that should matter at work."

There are many reasons why people choose to be in the closet at work, and there are many shades of being out. Some people choose to be out only to other gay people. Others will then "add on" those straight colleagues who are known to be gay-friendly. Still others are out to everyone. Learning from people who have taken all of these varied paths, and discovering the impact their decisions have had on their professional lives, is the equivalent of having access to a library of highly specialized career resources.

In my research, I found that people who are out of the closet in diverse and welcoming environments reported a substantial financial benefit. As a group, lesbians and gay men who are out to everyone within welcoming environments earn 50 percent more than their peers who describe themselves as being "totally closeted" ($91,500 versus $61,000). In addition to higher salaries, people in this group also report greater overall levels of job satisfaction, healthier and more productive relationships with colleagues and bosses, and increased opportunities for promotion.

When the first phase of my research was complete, I was interviewed by *The Advocate* about the benefits of being out at work. The writer asked me why being out within an affirming work environment translates into more salary dollars. My answer then and now remains the same: "As a member of the gay community, you will work better, be happier, and grow professionally when you are accepted and valued for you."

When you're part of an organization that believes who you are as an individual is a contributing factor to their success, you're more likely to achieve. The personal security that comes with the freedom to be yourself will further engage you in your work and, therefore, propel you forward in your career, and feeling like you're able to utilize all of your strengths will empower you to be more creative, energetic, and dedicated. On the other hand, when your employer isn't supportive of who you are as a human being, you can expect the opposite result.

TALKING ABOUT . . . FEELING LIKE YOU MATTER

When I began to interview people one-on-one, I was overwhelmed by the hospitality so many people demonstrated by inviting me to their homes for an interview over lunch, dinner, or, in Sharla's case, afternoon tea. At the time of our first interview, Sharla, thirty-one, was employed as an insurance investigator in Hermosa Beach, California. The company did not include sexual orientation in their diversity statement, nor did they provide domestic partner benefits. Out of the closet only to other gay people and a few select colleagues known to be gay-friendly, she shared with me her feelings toward her employer. "Sometimes I'll read about the company supporting charities or national organizations that I know discriminate against the gay community and it makes me furious. I think, 'Here I am, busting my butt to do a good job, which, by the way, increases company profits, and here they are taking money I helped them earn and giving it to people who want me to drop dead because of my sexual orientation.' Those are the days I usually go home early or take an extra long lunch. To be honest, it makes me much less engaged in my work, because obviously they don't care how their actions affect me."

For several hours on a rainy Saturday afternoon in Sharla's kitchen, our conversation always came back to how important it is to feel like you matter. The week before we met, Sharla had her annual review at work and was disappointed with the results. "My raise next year is going to be almost nonexistent," she told me. Then, looking down at her cup of tea, she offered some insight into why her review didn't yield a better outcome. "I know I haven't given it my all this year, but I thought it wouldn't make such a big difference. It's really hard to get excited about a company that isn't excited about me."

As we talked further about her current situation, and why it might be time for her to look for a new employer that does value her unique identity, she shared with me a great analogy. "I remember being in junior high and having a really hard time speaking in front of the class. My social studies teacher knew I was scared to death and took me aside to tell me she was counting on me to show the other kids how to do an assignment right. I'm sure it was total bull, but it worked. The inspiration and assurance I felt because of her belief in me gave me the courage to stand up in front of the entire class and believe in my own ability. I felt like I had something to offer, and that's really what it's all about." Taking the last sip of tea from her cup, she added, "I want to have a boss like that social studies teacher. If I worked for a company that made me feel like I really mattered, I'd be the happiest and most productive employee in the entire company."

Maximizing your potential for success requires you to give 100 percent, and it's simply not possible to do that if you're angry with your employer. And, by the way, it's not wrong to be angry at an employer that doesn't support or value who you are. In order to achieve and reach your highest possible level of success, you have to feel that you're valued and that you matter.

Giving Yourself Authority to Make Changes

One of the greatest rewards associated with conducting research over a fairly lengthy period of time is learning about positive changes that have happened in people's lives. Almost two years after my afternoon tea with Sharla, I was delighted to find out she had a new job and a new belief in her professional future. "The hardest part for me was committing to change." Making the decision to find a workplace where she would feel supported

You don't need anyone's permission to find an employer who believes in the unique value you bring to the world of work.

and valued, she interviewed with several potential employers and, in her words, "found the greatest success to date in my professional life." Now, in her new job as a claims officer with a leading HMO, she's part of an organization that actually recruits within the gay community, offers inclusive benefits, and even has a gay employee resource group. When I asked how her life has changed since the last time we met, she said, "It's amazing how much better I feel about myself overall—at work and at home. And I never spend time thinking about how to get out of work. That's a perk I've never had before."

Three Empowering Truths

Overcoming the impact of prejudices and bigotry begins by replacing old lies with new, empowering truths. Begin incorporating these three empowering truths into your professional belief system; make them your mantra, and never allow yourself to believe in the falsehoods of homophobia again. Remember that prejudice and bigotry will never produce the truth because they're built entirely on a foundation of ignorance and hate.

- **Truth #1:** I do not have to accept less in my career because of my sexual orientation.

- **Truth #2:** I have the authority to define my own value.

- **Truth #3:** I am fully empowered to find a professional environment where I can achieve and succeed as myself.

Write them down, say them out loud, and anchor them into your consciousness. Make these three empowering truths your guiding principles. Now, why are these your truths? Because you're as valuable as everyone else in the world. Gay people, in virtually all career fields and stages of their professional development, can be out of the closet and successful as themselves. Creating a career where who you are and what you do are in total harmony is possible. Believe in the value of your identity and your right to incorporate all of your individual strengths into your professional life.

Integrating Your Sexual Orientation into Your Career

Spending time at work considering whether or not your behavior is gender appropriate is a waste of your time and energy. Practically speaking, when you're free to be yourself at work, you have more time to devote to traveling your own road to success. You also gain a sense of confidence that enhances your job performance. And if you're concerned about the possibility of being "outed" by a colleague or client, then the time you spend worrying about how that scenario might actually unfold is counterproductive to your professional development. Integrating your sexual orientation into your overall identity at work will enable you to be who you are without fear of harassment or discrimination because you're gay.

TALKING ABOUT . . . BEING YOURSELF

For three years after he graduated from college, Art worked for a large financial firm where he constantly felt the need to monitor himself for what he described as "feminine" behavior. Art's experience mirrors the experiences of many other gay men, who often feel the need to be one of the "straight boys" in order to succeed. Today, at twenty-nine, he's out of the closet to everyone in his personal and professional life and employed in a position that's a model for lavender success, due in part to its welcoming and inclusive environment. However, his previous experience at a financial firm in Boston, Massachusetts, was very different.

"The people I worked with were primarily stereotypical frat-boy types, who still act the same way at thirty and forty as they did in college." Looking back on his experience, Art told me, "I'm not excusing myself, but when you're twenty-two and in denial about who you are sexually, going along with the in crowd at work can seem like the right thing to do." Still employed with the firm when he decided to come out in his personal life, he told me that he started to "watch" himself for any behavior at work that his colleagues might interpret as gay. "I can't believe how stupid I was to suddenly think I was going to become a different person." When I asked him what it was he was "watching," he said, "In some way I was 'acting' gay. And in my mind at that time, being gay was the equivalent of being effeminate. Part of my own coming out process was self-education, because I had a lot of preconceived notions about what it means to be gay."

Contrasting his work life now and then, Art talked about why he was miserable at the first firm. He describes his previous difficulties as a three-part problem. "The first part was my own personal conflict about accepting my sexual orientation. The second part was a homophobic company culture that reinforced my own negative self-image. The third part of the problem was something that's existed for eons, and it's that society allows the behavior of bigots to be acceptable under the 'right' circumstances." Art told me that when he finally "admitted" his sexual orientation to a few colleagues at the firm, he was ostracized. "It's funny," he said, "even using the word *admit* bothers me now, because it sounds like being gay is somehow bad, something you should hide."

Today, after nearly two years as assistant vice president of finance for a mortgage company, he finds himself less and less aware of anyone's behavior being masculine or feminine, gay or straight. "Once you get to the point where you're beyond one label being better or worse than another, the rest just falls into place. I've learned a lot about myself in the last two years. Particularly how destructive the culture in my previous job was to my own self-esteem. I didn't recognize the price I was paying in terms of my own mental health and personal relationships, because when you're mired down in bad circumstances, you have no frame of reference for how it's supposed to be. Now that I'm out at work and feeling good about it, I can tell you that there's no job title or amount of money that's worth giving up your own personal sense of freedom."

When you work for an organization that values people for themselves, you don't need to be anyone other than yourself.

Overcoming Workplace Labels

Nearly 75 percent of the people I interviewed who are closeted to some degree at work also monitor their on-the-job behavior in order to appear more "straight." In addition to changing "her" to "him" and vice versa when discussing their romantic lives, many people feel the need to act in ways they think are gender appropriate. In other words, many talented and skilled gay professionals are spending their emotional resources on matters that would be irrelevant if they had found the right job fit.

Art was absolutely on target when he said there's a toll paid for using your time and creative energies in ways that aren't part of your job. Worrying about the need to conform to traditional gender roles is not conducive to achievement. Never forget that you do not have to spend your professional capital taking on the characteristics of anyone other than yourself. When you base your road to success on the strength of your unique identity, you're free to pursue your dreams without altering what makes it all possible in the first place—you.

Fostering Communication and Achievement in the Workplace

Twenty-eight percent of the people in my study who are not out in the workplace left their last position because of isolation and loneliness. The benefits of being yourself extend beyond the opportunity to earn a higher salary and the ability to accomplish your day-to-day work. The denial of your sexual orientation can create communication barriers, since it is an innate human skill to detect insincerity, regardless of your motive. And because all workplaces are made up of communication networks, when you're disconnected, there's a tremendous struggle that goes on in order to be productive.

A fundamental requirement for effective communication in the workplace is mutual respect. Respect, in turn, produces trust. Regardless of your career field, good communication networks promote productive workplace relationships and are built on mutual respect and trust. When you are connected to this stream of information, you become empowered to succeed. In other words, when you place yourself in a position to access this steady stream of information, your job performance will be enriched because you're receiving relevant information and know more about the needs of the organization. You'll also be connected to your colleagues in a more personal and meaningful way, which, once again, can lead to tangible professional benefits including promotions, raises, and positive recognition.

TALKING ABOUT . . . COMMUNICATING AND CONNECTING AT WORK

Many closeted people find themselves disconnected from workplace communication networks for reasons that aren't related to the organization's culture. Even when people are employed in gay-friendly environments, a lack of self-acceptance and fear of coming out can prevent them from developing the types of relationships necessary for effective workplace communication.

Kay, a forty-five-year-old marketing manager in Los Angeles, works for a highly respected public university with a proven gay-friendly environment. In addition to its inclusive policies and diversity initiatives, there's an impressive list of out and successful gay people in senior positions. Still, Kay has made the decision not to be out at work.

When I first spoke with Kay to arrange an interview, she told me that she felt "stuck" in the same position after twelve years with her employer. "I don't know why I'm not further ahead," she said. "I work hard, get to work on time, but new people come in and move up, and I'm pretty much still where I started twelve years ago." Then she added something that explained why she was treading water instead of moving forward. "Maybe I just don't know how to play the political game as well other people. Sometimes I see the people I work with laughing and joking around, and I feel like an outsider." Trying her best to be indifferent about the situation, she said, "But after all, work is work, and I really don't have time to be buddy-buddy with people at work. It doesn't really matter if I'm part of the social environment or not."

Two weeks after our first conversation, Kay and I met in person at a coffeehouse near her office. As she shared the details of her personal background, I learned a great deal about her professional frustrations. For Kay, her inability to connect with her colleagues at work was linked to her own lack of self-acceptance. Married and divorced at an early age, she had led two lives since the age of twenty-seven. Even though her two grown children were now in college and out of the house, she was unable to break free from what she described as "feeling like I need to be someone else."

For the last ten years, Kay has had a life partner, who was also divorced and closeted at work. Even though they maintained separate households, Kay told me that since her children had moved out they spent most of their time together. As we talked about the toll of keeping so many segments of her life separated, she told me about the daily ritual she had developed for making the transition from work to home. "When I get in the car at night and pull out of the parking lot, I flip a mental switch and dim out the straight divorced woman I portray at the office. Then, by the time I get home, I'm ready to enter my 'real life' with my partner." There was a tremendous sense of sadness in her voice as she told me about how she shifts from one life to another. Kay also told me that she had spent most of her adult life feeling guilty about her sexual orientation. For Kay, feeling guilty about her own identity greatly contributed to her professional frustrations.

The by-product of staying in the closet is a loss of self-esteem. Spread out over time, this loss can go unnoticed until one day, like Kay, you question why you're not further ahead in your career. When you assume someone else's identity, you simultaneously give up incremental opportunities to communicate with others in your workplace in a clear, meaningful, and authentic voice. In other words, when someone feels like they hit a wall every time they talk to you because they can't quite figure out who you are, one of the fundamental requirements for communication that we discussed earlier, mutual trust, will not be met. Don't cheat yourself out of everything you deserve in your career because you've allowed the lies of prejudice and bigotry to permeate your life. Go back to your three empowering truths and never accept less because you're gay. Remember that being faithful to your identity will advance your career.

Banishing Fear and Guilt

When you spend 40 hours a week, fifty weeks a year, at work, you're looking at 2,000 hours on the job. In Kay's case, she spent 24,000 hours over twelve years portraying someone else. Over time, that staggering burden weighs heavily on your ability to succeed.

When I asked Kay what prevented her from coming out within an environment already proven to support members of the gay community, she didn't hesitate. "Fear and guilt," she said. "The fear of living my life in a way that's completely opposite of what I grew up thinking was the 'right' way to live. Plus the guilt I've always assumed as a mother and daughter, because I left a picket fence straight life for what I've been told is 'selfishness.' Having a straight identity at work, even if it's a lie, eases that guilt because it makes life easier for my parents and children." When I followed up with Kay more than a year later, she was still in the same job and continued to balance two identities. "Someday," she told me, "I'll be free to just live my life." I asked her when that day was going to come. "Probably when my parents are gone and I'm old enough to retire. Maybe at that point, it simply won't matter anymore."

● ● ●

Denying your authentic identity in the workplace lessens the effectiveness of your professional "voice" and leads to feelings of frustration, disconnection, and even complacency. When you're free to go to work as the same person you are when you get out of bed in the morning, you're able to clearly and consistently communicate the full value of who you are in your professional life. Being the same person before, during, and after work gives you the same freedom to pursue success as your straight colleagues. Enjoying professional equality, then, isn't only dependent on the culture of your workplace environment. True parity also requires that you grant yourself the freedom to succeed in your own skin.

Finding Workplace Freedom

EARLY ON IN MY RESEARCH, a registered letter marked "confidential" arrived from Jackson, a forty-five-year-old attorney in Los Angeles. Educated and extremely articulate, he detailed his struggle with his sexuality and the toll he believes it has taken on his professional life. His letter began with a very to-the-point diagram:

GAY + ALCOHOL = IMPACT ON CAREER

In his remarkably candid letter the link between how you feel about your sexual orientation and the impact those feelings have on your career was made immediately apparent. He wrote, "Alcohol destroyed my career, and much of my drinking started and continued because I was uncomfortable . . . with being gay." He started drinking heavily in high school and drank most heavily at boy-girl events. Throughout his undergraduate studies at an Ivy League university and continuing on through law school at USC, Jackson was always uncomfortable in social situations, and alcohol eased that discomfort. After law school, he continued to struggle with the same identity issues, only now, rather than a student, he was a "promising young attorney" with a well-known Los Angeles law firm. In the end, he said the feeling that he didn't deserve his own achievements overwhelmed him. "I finally realized my alcoholism after losing a wonderful job." Self-employed since he lost his job more than ten years ago, Jackson has had difficulty rebuilding his career because of his past reputation for drinking.

"It's been a long road back," he said, "both in terms of getting myself on track and embracing who I am. Who knows where I'd be in my career if I would've started off believing that being gay was okay."

Valuing Your Own Identity

Just as there is a connection between higher earnings and being out within a positive workplace environment, there is a connection between sustaining professional success and the value you place upon yourself as a human being. Almost everyone at some point has been told that it's inappropriate to brag about your own accomplishments. This message inspires in many a sense of doubt, causing them to question whether or not they are worthy of accomplishment in the first place. In other words, if you're unable to talk about how great you are, can it really be true? For many gay people, these doubts are exacerbated by the simultaneous message propagated by some that being gay is "bad." Many talented people I interviewed, for example, allowed their sense of self-doubt to negate the importance of all they've achieved.

TALKING ABOUT . . . YOUR PERSONAL VALUE

Lori is a twenty-seven-year-old pharmaceutical sales representative in Los Angeles who has incorporated the value of her unique identity into her personal and professional lives. "For me, I can't imagine having to switch gender labels when I talk to people at work about my lesbian friends or girlfriend." For Lori, the decision to acknowledge her sexual orientation was extremely personal. "Everyone has a favorite relative and my cousin Jay was that one special person. I thought he was the ultimate in cool, and to this day, I don't think I've ever seen a better-looking guy. Jay always looked out for me at family gatherings and made sure no one was picking on me for being a tomboy." Lori took a long pause before her next sentence. "A couple of days before his twenty-fifth birthday, he killed himself." Lori told me that two days before her cousin committed suicide, he came out to his parents and they rejected him. "When your parents tell you that you're less than nothing, it doesn't make you feel like you can go out and conquer the world. No one will ever convince me that his suicide was for any reason other than how he felt about his sexual orientation, even though his parents deny it to this day."

When I asked her how her cousin's suicide had changed her life, she said, "Even though we never talked about it and I was only fifteen when he killed himself, deep down he knew I was gay and vice versa. Looking back with adult eyes, that's why we were so close. There was this unspoken understanding about who the other one was, and in a way that always made me feel special. After he died, my mom pretty much broke off ties with my aunt because she couldn't stand the piety anymore. It also opened up the door to talk to my parents about my own sexual orientation." She said, "What happened to Jay scared the hell out of them, and they didn't want the same thing to happen to me." At the end of our interview, Lori summarized her feelings about her cousin's death in a very poignant way. "I decided the best way I could honor Jay is to be proud of who I am, and never become him. I think he would've been really pleased about the truthfulness of my life."

Finding the freedom to achieve as yourself in the world of work is directly connected to believing in the value of your own unique identity. When you affirm your own value and place yourself within a workplace environment that allows you to succeed as yourself, you grant yourself the freedom to excel. Finding workplace freedom doesn't have to be postponed or forfeited. You can create your own freedom, and you deserve nothing less.

EXERCISE **Describing the Professional Benefits of Workplace Freedom**

Consider the benefits you stand to gain when you begin to value your own unique identity. What role could workplace freedom play in how you approach your professional life? Your answers will create guidelines for your lavender road to success based on your own individual truths.

1. *What positive feelings do you associate with the word freedom?*

2. *If you are currently employed at a homophobic workplace, how would your approach to your job and how you feel about yourself be different if suddenly it became a gay-friendly environment?*

3. *List three professional goals you want to accomplish in your career. Can you be as effective or reach the same level of success if you aren't free to tap into the entire strength of your identity?*

When you choose to work within an organization that empowers you to succeed based on who you are, you set yourself up to experience freedom. If you're currently unable to be yourself at work, examine your answers to question two above. You'll likely find that your "new" approach to work would foster many of the positive feelings you associated with the word *freedom*. Finally, ask yourself if your three goals could be accomplished more quickly if you were completely free to be yourself at work.

Coming Out at Work

Coming out at work can be liberating and terrifying. The experience can also be full of irony. In Jim's case, it was all three. A thirty-five-year-old new media executive in Los Angeles, he made the decision to come out three months after joining the company. "I really wanted to do this right," he told me, "and decided to talk to my boss before anyone else. I'd never been totally out at work before, and finally came to the conclusion that I was wasting too much time keeping up the charade." He laughed, "I even started to think of myself as a budding activist, which is really a stretch for me." After evaluating the gay-friendliness of the company, a process he describes as "finding out the real deal," he began rehearsing his coming out speech. "I thought of a million different scenarios, but never imagined such a crazy ending." Jim said that when he first interviewed with his boss, he thought he might actually be gay himself until he mentioned his ex-wife. "It never seemed appropriate to ask, but from time to time I just had this feeling that maybe he was gay, too."

Jim planned every detail. "First, I was going to talk about how great it is that the company is so inclusive, and then talk more specifically about gay diversity. I planned to drop a few hints about my own life and then act like it was totally unimportant as I casually mentioned that my lover and I were planning to buy a new house. That was going to be my way of easing into coming out." But it didn't work out that way. Jim unintentionally outed himself during a business lunch with his boss and two clients he'd never met before. "We were meeting with two well-known software designers and talking about a new product that had just come on the market. My partner, Todd, had been having a lot of success using the product in his own work, and I suddenly heard myself blurt that fact out over lunch. I think my own need to come out was so great that it was just bubbling there, waiting to jump out of my mouth!" Jim said that he was expecting some type of gasp or reaction but got nothing. "All that angst, and it was like I'd announced that I had eaten a bagel for breakfast. Then, after about five awkward minutes of watching them look back and forth at each other and smirking, they all started to laugh. It turns out that not only is my boss gay, but the two women are lovers. All I can say is that my 'gaydar' gene must totally be out of order!"

People who make the decision to come out within a workplace determined to be welcoming—regardless of their age, profession, or industry—have overwhelmingly positive results. Many people told me that being gay was a much bigger issue for them than it was for colleagues and employers. Others learned that their sexual orientation wasn't really a secret after all. But beyond the reactions of their employers and coworkers, the outcome that mattered most was the sense of freedom and enhanced self-value that was gained. More than 90 percent of those who came out within welcoming environments told me they have never felt better about themselves and about going to work.

When you feel good about who you are as an individual, you're going to feel that you deserve to succeed as yourself.

In order to realize these positive outcomes, it's necessary first to assess how receptive your workplace will be. Many people told me they made a conscious effort to establish themselves as qualified members of the organization before coming out. Others felt so strongly about being out from the very first day on the job that they came out during the interview process. The decision to come out within a homophobic or gay-hostile environment, however, should be approached with caution and a great deal of consideration. Becoming a victim of workplace harassment or violence is not the goal. Later in this chapter we'll address how to determine the potential for successfully coming out within any given workplace environment.

TALKING ABOUT . . . COMING OUT BEFORE YOU START A JOB

When you're hired as yourself, you feel good about who you are and about the organization that hired you. The wisdom I heard expressed most often by people who were out of the closet during their job search was that their offer of employment served to reinforce their decision to be themselves.

Nick, a thirty-eight-year-old studio executive in Los Angeles, left a large international consulting firm after being denied partner status because of his sexual orientation. When I spoke with Nick to set up an interview, he invited me to meet for lunch at the studio's commissary. As a senior member of the studio's business affairs unit, he works with agents, writers, and producers to put projects together for both television and movies. The current state of his professional life is light-years away from his previous position. About his time at the consulting firm, he said, "I thought I'd done a good job hiding my sexual orientation. Like a lot of gay men I know in the consulting field, I always brought a female date to company events. I felt that 'don't ask, don't tell' was the right way to go in my career. When I didn't get promoted to partner after seven years of successful employment, I was determined to find out why. Finally, a friend of mine who happened to be at the meeting where my fate was decided reluctantly told me that one of the senior partners said I was 'too effeminate' to represent the company at the next level."

Nick told me that the devastation he felt eventually led to a hospital stay for stomach ulcers. At that point, he made the decision to leave the firm and find a job where he no longer had to hide his sexual orientation. "When I started looking for a new job, I realized that one of the reasons I stayed in the same place for seven years was because I was afraid to go anywhere else. When I realized I had to get out, basically to save my own health, the first thing I did was look at companies that were known for supporting diversity. I realized that, for the most part, the big consulting firms just weren't on that list. But instead of getting more depressed, it was like this big dark cloud that had hovered over my life went away. Not having that option meant that I wasn't going to be in the consulting field anymore, which, to be honest, felt like getting a stay of execution. I didn't know where I was going when I got out, but I knew I was going to be free. One thing I did know for certain was that I wasn't going to spend my workday at a company where I had to change my personality to suit some ridiculous homophobic standard."

After a four-month job search in a difficult economy, Nick accepted his current position in the entertainment industry along with a 15 percent increase in pay. "There are a lot of similarities between what I do now and what I used to do in the sense that I solve problems. In many ways I guess

I'm still a consultant helping other people do business in a more effective way. But the big difference is the environment and the people I work with." I asked him what he felt was the biggest difference between his professional life then and now. "It feels like it's my career now. Plus, instead of flying all over the place like I used to do, I get to stay home and have a life." I asked Nick how he felt when he received the offer from his new employer since he had been out of the closet throughout the interview process. "In a weird way, it was so good it made me a bit uncomfortable. I'd been so accustomed to hiding that I was afraid to really be myself. But going to work that first day, knowing I didn't have to worry about someone thinking I was, might be, or could be gay, and what effect that would have on my career, was worth everything I had to go through to get here. The peace of mind is amazing."

Achieving More by Being Yourself

My conversation with Melinda was filled with laugher. She has an incredible sense of humor and a sarcastic wit that she admits is part of her own professional survival package. "Because I'm a woman and a nurse, I'm supposed to be empathetic, sympathetic, all those 'pathetic' words! My patients say that I entertain while I heal." At forty-four, Melinda has worked for a large HMO in California's San Fernando Valley for more than fifteen years. She's out in her personal life, but closeted at work. "When I started my career, it wasn't politically correct to be gay at work." She said, "To tell you the truth, in some ways I honestly think I'm less out today than I was twenty years ago, because I've come to believe that most of the straight world is homophobic and I just don't want to deal with it." In the past twenty years, Melinda has had two employers and has not advanced to where she expected to be at this point in her life. She told me that her first job out of nursing school was at a private hospital in Los Angeles, where an older doctor suggested that she needed to be more "womanly." She said, "I know I shouldn't have let that influence how I live my life at work, but it did. For the entire five years I worked there, I concentrated really hard on being what the world wanted me to be. I even convinced myself that I was straight long enough to get engaged for about two seconds! Then, when I took my next job, which is where I still am today, it never dawned on me to consider being out at work or that I even had a choice."

In the past fifteen years Melinda has been promoted only once. Although she's received annual salary increases, she told me that even in conjunction with her promotion, her highest increase to date has been 5 percent and they average 2–3 percent annually. I asked her how this compares with others in her organization and she told me that colleagues with less experience typically receive an annual increase of 5 percent or more. "I know they always give me less because I accept less. Sometimes I get really down on myself, because I do struggle financially compared to where I'd like to be in my life. But then those days pass, and I just keep on doing what I'm doing."

Melinda has quietly accepted less because she isn't using the full strength derived from her power source—her unique identity. In her case, being in the closet at work has taken a quiet toll on her self-esteem. Almost twenty years into her career, she doesn't feel valuable enough as an individual to seek "full-value" compensation in her career. When you're free to be yourself and feel good about who you are, you'll have the personal authority to command a higher salary.

Living in the Truth

Living life as yourself means that you're living in the truth. Why do we lie? Sometimes it's because we're unhappy with our situation and want to create an artificial reality that we perceive as better. But if that artificial reality requires denying your unique identity, it's time to stop and look at the value of your truth. You don't have to hide in the workplace.

TALKING ABOUT . . . BEING IN THE CLOSET

Martin, seventy-three, is a retired educator who began his career as a teacher in the late 1940s and waited until retirement to come out to his colleagues. His reason for waiting until he was no longer working was due to a very real fear. "All through my career I was a single, closeted gay man and knew if I were 'found out' I'd probably lose my job." The advancement of equal rights for the gay community and the opportunity to come out successfully at work have increased substantially since Martin began his career. After he retired, thinking he was leaving his career in education behind, he finally felt he had the freedom to come out to his colleagues. Ironically, the personal strength he gained by coming out has actually led him to a rewarding post-retirement career as a speaker and writer working to prevent gay-related hate crimes in public schools. "These are very encouraging times in spite of the strong control of the religious reactionaries. We haven't won the battle for equal rights and much is yet to be accomplished. I have worked with high school students who were gaybashed and know firsthand how cruel people can be in the name of selfrighteousness. Our strength is being ourselves and openly honest, as well as being an example for others to appreciate. As a community, we have contributed much to the improvement of the world and need to support each other in making sure we never have to go back into the closet."

EXERCISE **Five Steps to Workplace Freedom**

Why is it so important in your career to travel a truthful road? Because it's simply not possible to achieve your highest success in the world of work in the shoes of someone who doesn't exist. No matter how honorable or reasonable your motives for being untruthful about your identity may be, including an environment that prevents you from being yourself, there will be a point where a toll is taken on your career and your life. Creating your own workplace freedom involves placing yourself in an organization that values your unique identity, setting goals for coming out, and developing an approach that reflects the realities of the organization. The following five steps will help you navigate the process of coming out at work.

1. List five professional and personal benefits you seek to realize by coming out at work. By articulating these benefits, you'll increase your motivation to achieve your goal of workplace freedom.

2. List five pros and five cons of being out of the closet at your workplace. This will give you a snapshot of the environmental realities associated with your workplace and help you decide if the organization is worthy of your time, effort, and talent.

3. Assess your answers. Do you have more pros than cons? Or do the negatives outweigh the positives? If you have more cons than pros, then coming out may never bring you true freedom because of antigay sentiments in your workplace. If you're in this position, don't worry. When you've completed this book you'll have the tools and resources necessary to find a workplace that will give you the opportunity to succeed as yourself.

4. Identify three personal advocates who believe in your right to succeed as yourself and will support you through the process of coming out at work. It's important to have support from people outside the organization with whom you can share your feelings without worrying about workplace politics.

5. Now identify the people within the organization, regardless of their position, whom you believe will be the most receptive to your decision to attain workplace freedom. Organizational hierarchy has much less to do with successfully coming out at work than making sure that your initial audience is open-minded and understanding. Don't feel that you need to come out first to your boss if she or he isn't on the list.

Once you've come out to the people on your list, you'll acquire additional support, energy, and personal authority to handle those who may not be as receptive. And never forget that your personal advocates are right there beside you, cheering you on to workplace freedom.

Supporting the Coming Out Process of Others

Helping others realize their own workplace freedom is one of the best investments you'll ever make. The rewards are far-reaching and can be achieved simply by being yourself. You may never know the extent to which your choice to live life in your own skin impacts others in a positive way. From a big picture perspective, by coming out you'll be contributing to the extinction of homophobia and bigotry. From a more personal perspective, you'll be contributing to the betterment of the day-to-day lives not only of gay people, but also of anyone who may be told they aren't deserving of success because of who they are in the world.

James Stofan, director of alumni affairs for the University of California system, which includes both UC Berkeley and UCLA, told me he believes that as more people experience the freedom to come out in the workplace, there will be a correlating need to expand the role of gay alumni groups. "The ability to see other gay people who are out and successful in their jobs communicates a powerful and positive message. Gay alumni groups are the most logical resource to meet that need." Out and successful in his own career, James has distinguished himself in the field of higher education by pursuing his own dreams as himself. "Currently, there isn't a national organization that connects gay alumni groups from different universities together as a whole. And when you consider that each year there are approximately two million new college graduates in this country alone, and if you accept that at least 10 percent of those graduates are gay, there's enough networking power to render homophobia obsolete. When you realize that within the University of California system alone there's potentially a group of 100,000 gay alumni, it's clear that the opportunity to provide role models to let others know that you can be gay and prosperous in your career is immense."

● ● ●

Gay people are succeeding as themselves every day in the world of work. You can create your own workplace freedom by working for people who believe in who you are as a unique individual. Consider the following question. If you're going to support an organization with your time, talent, and hard work, shouldn't you be supported as well?

When you feel like you can't be yourself in the workplace, you don't possess the basic requirements you need to succeed. Several people told me their initial approach was to beat homophobic employers at their own game, but pretending to be someone an employer wants you to be in order to succeed doesn't work in the long run. You simply can't sustain success or reach your highest plateaus if you're wearing someone else's suit.

Finally, you don't have to come out of the closet today, or feel like you've done something wrong if you are in the closet at work. It's okay to be just where you are right now. But what can you do today? You can acknowledge that freedom in the workplace is already enjoyed by others and you can believe in your professional value. You deserve to pursue your career and your dreams as yourself.

Increasing Your Professional Value

How many times have you been at a social gathering and almost before you were in the door someone asked, "What do you do?" The answer to this question has become so ingrained in how we define ourselves that our job titles seem more important than who we are as people. A few weeks after my interview with Keri, a thirty-nine-year-old attorney for the city of New York, she called to say she was coming to L.A. and suggested we get together for lunch. At the end of our original phone interview we had talked for more than an hour about a variety of business and political issues facing the gay community. Because we had such a "meeting of the minds" I was really looking forward to continuing our conversation in person. When we met, it was like getting together with an old friend.

The previous night, Keri had attended a dinner honoring one of her college mentors. She had an interesting experience related to the "what do you do" question. "I was standing in line at the dessert buffet and this buttoned-down guy with monogrammed cuff links, a diamond watch, and a fake tan asked me in a really snotty voice, 'So, what firm are you with?' His tone left no question in my mind that there was a right and wrong answer. I guess my off-the-rack business suit and fifty dollar watch screamed 'public defender' and it bothered me. So I looked him straight in the eye and proudly told him I was a public defender for the people of New York City."

Keri told me she expected the man to walk away when he found out she wasn't with a prestigious law firm. However, because she announced her profession and employer with pride and self-assurance, the "buttoned-down guy" started to ask her all kinds of questions about her day-to-day work. "I figured when I told him I was a public defender and didn't have any famous clients, he'd immediately move on to someone he perceived as having more professional value. But I was wrong. He was genuinely interested in what I do." Keri told me they talked for quite a long time. "I think I even opened his mind to some new thoughts and perspectives about our field of law." Because Keri wasn't the least bit hesitant about what she does for a living, she was able to communicate the value that she placed on her profession. Had she been perceived as being embarrassed by her job, the encounter would have likely had a different outcome. When you're engaged in your work and proud of what you do, you become an active participant in creating your own success.

Passion about your work facilitates achievement because it increases your professional value.

Committing to the Truth of Your Gender Identity

Creating a career based on your true identity requires commitment. When I began my research, one of my goals was to discover the level of workplace bias against those who self-identify as transgender compared to those who identify themselves as gay or lesbian. I asked both groups specific questions about the attitudes of bosses and supervisors as well as workplaces in general. What I found was that the perceived level of bias toward people who are transgender is nearly three times higher than for people who are gay or lesbian. Finding a workplace environment where you're afforded the opportunity to succeed as yourself is much more difficult.

TALKING ABOUT . . . GENDER IDENTITY

Perhaps more than most, Michelle, a thirty-eight-year-old woman who is transgender, has overcome great odds to live her life with truth and dignity. When I first interviewed Michelle, she was in the middle of a very difficult period of employment as an accounts manager at a bank in Southern California's San Fernando Valley. "It was clear to me from the first day I stepped foot in the bank, no one wanted me to be there." Prior to arriving at this particular branch, Michelle had been successfully employed by the same bank for six years in San Francisco. "I guess I was naive to think I could leave the Bay Area and work in an atmosphere where I wasn't considered an oddity."

Michelle told me that she thought her major struggle after transferring to Southern California to take care of her mother was going to be coping with her mother's illness. "I just hadn't planned on the level of hate and anger directed toward me—both from customers and other employees at the bank." She told me that few of the comments were made simply out of ignorance, and most were lewd. Several incidents, including a customer's threat of physical assault in the bank's parking lot, led her to file a report with the police. "The police were more helpful than the bank, but until someone actually does something to you, it's hard to get any protection. Then, it's too late."

In the midst of balancing the extremely difficult environment at work with her role as primary caregiver at home, Michelle found support from leaders of the bank's gay employee resource group in San Francisco. "I didn't want to give up and just quietly go away. I'd invested too much time with the company and worked too hard on becoming the person I was truly meant to be in this world." At the same time, however, Michelle was afraid for her life. "Hate crimes against the transgender community are out of control and I didn't want to become another statistic."

Eight months later I spoke with Michelle. After intense talks with corporate headquarters, Michelle was offered an equivalent position at a branch office in West Hollywood, California. She told me, "It wasn't the perfect solution because my mother's house is five minutes from the location in the Valley, but I'm able to keep my job and go to work without wondering if today is going to be the day that something terrible happens." Michelle told me that she never missed a day of work throughout the whole ordeal, and on her last day of work in the Valley she walked out at the close of business with her head held high. "I never once compromised my integrity or my work and it feels like my career is back on track because once again it's okay to be me." Based on the results of my research, her assessment of her experience is accurate. "I was luckier than most," Michelle said. "A lot of my transgender friends in similar circumstances have had no support from their employers. Several people were fired. It's sad to think that people care more about what you look like than what you can do."

Engaging in Your Career

Having counseled and coached more than a thousand college students and professionals at all stages of their careers, I've never heard anyone say, "I'd really like to work for a company that I'm ashamed of." Nor have I heard, "I'd really like to be buried under more piles of work, and be more stressed out."

Similarly, the vast majority of people I interviewed for this book are looking for professional lives that don't require them to hide, lie, or expend valuable energy pretending they're someone other than themselves. They also want to have a job that means something to them, energizes them, and gives them a reason to get up in the morning full of anticipation and joy at the prospect of going to work. When you're connected to your career at a deeper level, with honesty and a sense of pride about what you do, you'll be more productive and realize a greater overall sense of professional satisfaction.

TALKING ABOUT . . . ENGAGING IN YOUR CAREER

Sheila and her partner, Anne, both thirty-one, live in Atlanta. Sheila is a successful hospital administrator in the city and is out of the closet at work. Anne is a communications officer for a bank in a suburb twenty miles outside Atlanta. Anne is closeted at work. Sheila says she loves her job and feels valued by her employer. In contrast, Anne does not have the freedom to be out at work, and, as a result, she isn't as engaged in her career or her professional future as her partner.

When I first met Sheila and Anne, I asked them about their experiences with homophobia in the workplace as it related to their geographic location. According to Sheila, "I think it's just a matter of common sense. I mean, I'm a lesbian in the South, and if you want to be safe you can only live and work where there's some type of liberal influence. I'm a dyed-in-the-wool left-wing Democrat and will only work where I believe my own political party is in the majority. That's my golden rule for successful employment in the South." She said, "Atlanta certainly isn't Manhattan or San Francisco, but in Georgia, it's the big city. And it's your best bet if you're gay."

Anne's philosophy was very different. "I don't think about my career the same way as Sheila. I like to get comfortable with a routine and stick to it. Familiarity means more to me than moving up the ladder." Anne described most of her colleagues as either born-again Christians or extremely conservative. She said, "I couldn't even think about coming out if I wanted to keep my job."

I was curious about whose career was the focus of discussion at home, and Sheila and Anne confirmed my guess. "Without a doubt, it's mine," Sheila said. "Even when we're out to dinner with our gay friends, Anne doesn't say much about her work, other than 'it's fine.' At night, when I ask her about her day, it's always 'same old, same old.'"

In response to Sheila's comments, Anne said, "I get up, go to work, and come home—like everybody else in the world. Sure, life could be better, but it's good enough for me. I figure I could always be in a worse spot than I am now." Whether Anne's lack of interest in her career is a result of her not being valued at work or whether she simply doesn't rate work as a priority can't be known until she makes a change in her workplace environment. But even if your career isn't a high priority, your life will be greatly enriched when you're an active participant rather than a bystander at work.

A year and a half later I checked in again with Sheila and Anne. The situation remained basically the same, although I sensed Sheila's growing frustration with Anne's reluctance to make a professional change. She summed up the reason for her partner's lack of career enthusiasm with the following insight. "I am who I am twenty-four hours a day, seven days a week. Anne has to be two people, and I don't think she likes the closeted nine-to-five woman as much as she likes the woman that I love at home. It's tough on her all day being around people who exhibit such ignorance about gay people. I want her to want more for herself." In her own quiet way, Anne agreed.

Giving Yourself the Right to Thrive

When your work life and personal values come together, aligning who you are with what you do, your career becomes an expression of your values, talents, skills, personality, and sexual orientation. When this alignment occurs, you're then able to fully utilize your unique identity. As a result, you become energized by your work because you're actively contributing to your professional future.

Settling for less always leaves an aftertaste of loss. It's a bit like getting five numbers instead of six in the lottery. You've almost won, but not quite. And the "not quite" makes all the difference in the world. Of course, the main difference between the lottery and your career is that you don't have to rely on the luck of the draw. You have the ability to pick the right employer and win at work. What many people don't realize is that when their job is "just good enough," it actually isn't. There's a big difference between "surviving" and "thriving."

TALKING ABOUT . . . THRIVING AT WORK

Ken is a thirty-three-year-old design engineer living and working in Phoenix, Arizona. Prior to choosing his current employer, a gay-friendly technology firm with fifty employees, he worked for a much larger and nationally known aerospace company. He described his previous employer as having a "don't ask, don't tell" culture.

It isn't enough just to survive in your professional life—you deserve to thrive.

"I never lied about being gay when directly asked, but I avoided that question at all costs. It wasn't a place where you'd feel comfortable being out of the closet." Although he never experienced any type of on-the-job harassment, Ken told me he often felt uncomfortable around certain colleagues. "I just knew who had a problem with my sexual orientation and it was awkward when I had to work closely with them because I knew they didn't want to work with someone who's gay." He added, "I hated to call on them for help. It always made me feel like I was begging for scraps."

Over a five-year period Ken received good reviews and felt his overall compensation was fair. However, the year prior to his leaving he was discouraged from applying for a promotion. "I'll never know for sure, but had I been straight, I think I would've been encouraged to at least get in the running. My gut tells me it was because the position had two direct reports that were long-term employees that I knew were homophobic. I'm almost certain that's why I was subtly told to forget it." He paused for a moment, then said, "Not having a chance was demeaning."

Ken told me that there was something missing even before he was turned down as a candidate for the promotion. "Sometimes I'd come home from work and almost feel like I'd done something wrong all day. It took me a long time to figure it out. The reason I felt like I had done something wrong was that I always accepted what was given to me just because it seemed 'good enough.' I finally got tired of things being just good enough."

Through a networking association for professionals in his field, Ken learned about a new company that was adding staff. "It was really exciting to think about having a job where my ideas mattered more than my sexual orientation. Now, after a little more than two years, I'd say I've contributed twice as much as I did in my previous job, and I was there for five years." I asked him how he feels when he comes home from work. He said, "Now I always feel like my day was well spent. Even when something's gone wrong, I know it's about the work and not me as a person. There's a sense of calmness in my life that didn't exist until now."

Enhancing Your Strength through Cross-Cultural Alliances

For the past several years I've attended an annual awards dinner honoring standout employers who support the gay community in the workplace. One of the awards is always presented to someone straight who has supported gay employees. That award is an important reminder that there are vast numbers of business leaders who do get it.

The first year I went to the dinner, the award went to an accomplished senior vice president of human resources for a Fortune 500 company who knew exactly what it was like to be considered less deserving by certain segments of society. An African-American woman who began her career in the late 1960s when she left college, she overcame oppression and discrimination to achieve her professional dreams. That night, as she accepted her award, she talked about how she went against the wishes of several top executives to gain support within the company to add sexual orientation to their equal opportunity employment policy in the 1990s. She opened her speech by saying, "I knew in my heart it was the right thing to do, and in all the years since, I've never once doubted my commitment to the gay community." Seeking support from leaders of the company's black employee resource group she was told by the president of the group that gay people didn't need to be protected, and, furthermore, she shouldn't be helping "those people." Her reply to him spoke directly to the heart of workplace diversity. Not one to mince words, she asked him if he ever heard anyone called "fag" or "dyke" or "queer" while at work. He told her that he had. Her response was powerful. She said, "If you don't stand up for the dignity of other people, how long do you think it will be before people start to think it's okay to be just as nasty and vulgar toward you because of who you are?" The very next day she had the support of his group, and other minority-based employee groups soon followed.

As our community continues to move forward, it's important to remember that we have the support of many great business and political leaders. In turn, in order for us to continue the progress we've already achieved, it is imperative that we become allies with others who may face workplace discrimination because of their unique identities. Supporting the workplace rights of others, and therefore ourselves, requires crossing racial, economic, and religious borders. Even within our own community, it's vital to our professional and political health to support each other based on our shared diversity. Listen with an open mind, take the feelings of others seriously, show respect for people, and keep in mind that your own opportunity for success is connected to the opportunities enjoyed by other minority communities.

When you support the human rights of others, you're not only doing the right thing, you're also reinforcing your own rights.

Creating Ambition with Positive Energy

Believing in your inherent value as a gay human being is one of the most important steps on your road to success. Having a positive outlook on what you can accomplish in the world of work isn't something that just happens. You must intentionally develop and maintain the positive energy that keeps you motivated. When you incorporate into your life people who are achieving in their own careers, you'll be taking action to move yourself closer to your goals. The next time you're at work, take a look around when it's time to go to lunch and notice who's sharing a table. Quite often, people who make complaining about their difficulties a full-time job will bond at work. Similarly, people who are focused on achieving will also bond at work. It's not always corporate hierarchy that draws people together over lunch or at the watercooler. To a great extent, it's about shared levels of ambition. In other words, if you're dedicated to making your professional

Building alliances and supporting others in their quest for workplace equality will enhance your own lavender road to success.

dreams come true, surround yourself with people who are on the same path. It's energizing to be around people who are excited about their futures. Likewise, the constant cynicism and blighted hope of people who live to complain can cause you to veer from your road to success and plant seeds of doubt in your mind about your own value and abilities. Now, I'm not suggesting that you clean house and cut out of your life anyone who isn't ambitious and charismatic. What I am suggesting is that positive energy creates positive energy, and you want to take advantage of that dynamic. When you incorporate into your life people who believe in themselves and their own dreams, their ambition will motivate you to move forward in your own career.

EXERCISE **Who Influences My Energy?**

It's vital to develop an awareness of the energy that surrounds those you associate with at work and in your personal life.

1. List the five people you spend the most time with at work and the five you spend time with when you're not at work. How are these people contributing to your road to success?

2. Ask yourself these five questions about the people on your list:

   • Are they generally positive about their own future and mine?
   • How do I feel before, during, and after our interactions?
   • Do I feel free to share my career dreams with them?
   • Are they supportive of my dreams or do they shoot down my ideas?
   • Do I respect their opinions and consider their feedback valuable?

Developing Leadership Skills

Leadership is a skill that you can acquire that will help you succeed in any role in an organization. In fact, being a leader has much more to do with having confidence in your own abilities and being responsive to the emotional climate of the organization than it does with job titles and corporate hierarchy.

As I've already mentioned, being out at work provides you with a multitude of benefits, including a higher salary, increased job satisfaction, and a greater likelihood of advancement. You'll also enjoy more opportunities to cultivate leadership behaviors that factor back into your road to success.

In other words, developing leadership behaviors will facilitate your own achievement because they enhance your professional value.

One of the most exciting aspects of my research has been the professional diversity of the gay alumni from USC. From teachers to attorneys to entrepreneurs, gay USC grads are represented in virtually every career field and industry. Those members of the gay community who are out of the closet and have advanced in their careers to occupy typical leadership roles share four common characteristics: they are credible, effective, innovative, and likable. Wherever you are in your profession today, choosing to develop these leadership behaviors will serve you extremely well on your road to success.

When you know how your unique identity provides you with professional advantages, who you are becomes a valuable asset.

- **Be credible:** Follow through on commitments and never overstate your abilities.

- **Be effective:** Understand the mission of the organization and do all you can to ensure that your own work contributes to that mission.

- **Be innovative:** Create new ways to accomplish your work and solve problems within the scope of your job.

- **Be likable:** Recognize others in the workplace by listening to them and encouraging them in their own pursuits.

To identify these four leadership behaviors I specifically looked for people who had ten or more employees reporting to them, but let me repeat something I stated at the beginning of this section: leadership is not just reserved for CEOs or people with a staff. Leadership is about being responsive to the diverse personalities of individuals within the organization, and it exists at many levels. Your sexual orientation does not preclude you from being a leader.

In chapter 10, we'll explore how your life experiences as a result of being gay can enhance your ability to respond to the needs of others in the workplace. Your sexual orientation is your built-in competitive advantage, and it facilitates your ability to be a leader.

●●●

Your professional value is intrinsically linked to how you view yourself. And you communicate that value to other people through daily interactions and through your message, regardless of topic. Think about a leader that you admire and respect. Doesn't he or she exude a sense of self-worth and confidence in all that he or she does? Committing to your individual truth affords you the opportunity to excel because that commitment grounds you in your own value. Michelle, for example, would not have had the fortitude or courage to persevere if she hadn't believed in the value of her unique identity. You, too, are valuable because of who you are in the world. Recognize that reality and take that belief into the world of work. When you believe in yourself and your profession, there are no limits to what you can achieve.

Getting on the Right Road

WHEN I FIRST ARRIVED AT USC AS A FRESHMAN, I was overwhelmed with anxiety about whom I was going to live with in the dorms. My biggest fear was that I'd be rooming with a jock who had no need for a closeted sissy boy in his living quarters. The residence hall I was assigned to was called Touton Hall (pronounced "tootin"), otherwise known as Rootin' Tootin'. I waited until the very last minute to move in. Grappling with suitcases and boxes, I finally made the climb up the three flights of stairs to my room. When I opened the door I was relieved to find that although my new roommate had already moved in, he wasn't home. Looking around, I knew instantly that my worst fears had come true. My roommate was a football-playing, back-slapping frat boy! Now, some might say this was a good thing, but in my mind there was only one solution to this horrible situation—an off-campus apartment. I won't even go into the song and dance I gave my parents about why I had to live in a studio apartment all by myself, but somehow it worked. But on that very day, had I been able to look into the future, I would have been amazed at the progress that would be made in the world and where my own road would take me.

Twenty years later, Rootin' Tootin' has been torn down. All that remains is a plaque on the sidewalk noting where it once stood. Passing by on my way to a meeting recently, I stopped to read the plaque and reflect on my own history. Across the street from this spot I once approached with such trepidation there now stands a residence tower that's home to the university's Rainbow Floor, dedicated to affirming students' gay, lesbian, bisexual, or transsexual experience. Two decades earlier I never dreamed that such a change could take place.

Creating a Future That Represents Your Full Potential

Eleanor Roosevelt once said, "No one can ever make you feel inferior without your consent." When it comes to your career, those words could not be truer.

If you allow certain people to make you feel inferior because you're gay, you open the door to making career decisions that don't take advantage of your full potential. When you feel like you deserve the best, you'll create situations that result in your success.

TALKING ABOUT . . . YOUR FUTURE

Hands down, the most unusual setting of all of my interviews was New Orleans Square at Disneyland in Anaheim, California. When I called Andrew to arrange for an interview, I learned that we were both planning to visit the famed amusement park on the same day with relatives from out of town. Because of our travel and work schedules, we decided it would be easiest to meet at the park. After I bought a notepad and pen at one of the gift shops, we sat down amid wandering pirates and assorted Disney characters in New Orleans Square while our respective out-of-town guests entertained themselves on a ride. Andrew is a twenty-seven-year-old MBA student who earlier in his career chose not to follow his dreams because he didn't feel "an effeminate gay man would be able to succeed in the boardrooms of corporate America." At the time of our first interview, Andrew was employed with a gay-friendly health-care organization in Pasadena, California, as a human resources manager. He told me, "I like the company I work for, but I don't like what I do."

Andrew's dream has always been to lead the marketing division of a large corporation. As a teenager, he began working for his parents in a small gourmet fast-food restaurant. "I was the one who always had new ideas about how to reach more customers and make more money. When they saw that my ideas were working, they let me run with them." By the time Andrew graduated from high school, his family had opened several other successful locations. "Because I had already proven myself as a 'marketer,' I really wanted to do it on a larger scale." Even though he's always been out and affirming of who he is in the world, he bought into the mind-set that he could only be successful in what he calls "gay jobs." In fact, the primary reason he didn't pursue a business major in college was that he didn't think he would be valued in a traditional business environment. "My parents have always been supportive of me and I know I'm really lucky in that respect. In a way, my sexual orientation was overemphasized by my parents in terms of what would be available to me in the world." Andrew told me that when he began to apply for college with a declared major in business, his parents voiced concerns. "They felt the level of homophobia I'd face would be more prevalent in business than in other industries." He smiled as he now affirmed his own identity. "A friend of mine once told me that being in the closet was never an option for me, because even if you barricade the door, you can't hide the fact that I'm gay." He laughed as he added, "And I never want to hide. But I also feel like I've given a lot up because I've followed a narrower path." At the end of our first interview on the re-created Bourbon Street; we talked about his goals for the future. He said the first thing on his list was getting an MBA. "I want to accomplish my goals as a gay man in corporate America and I'm going to make it happen."

Two years later, almost to the day, Andrew and I met again. This time we were in a coffeehouse in Los Angeles. The first thing he said to me was, "I'm following my dream!" Returning to graduate school full-time to earn his MBA with an emphasis in marketing, he was excited about his professional future. "I know in some companies there's a 'lavender ceiling' or just outright homophobia, but those aren't companies I want to join. For me, if I don't go after what I want because I'm afraid of being mistreated, then I'm really giving up before I get started." Based on the progress he's already made, I'm confident that if we meet again in another two years Andrew will be well on his way to achieving his dream. At the end of our interview, we made a deal. When he's appointed the new "out and proud" marketing czar for corporate America, he's going to ask me to write his biography!

Recognizing the Right Road

Have you ever purchased an item of clothing because it looked so great on the model in the magazine that you thought you wanted the same look for yourself? Sometimes you'll recognize the wrong match in the dressing room. Other times an honest friend will call you on your decision. And, usually, their truthfulness isn't that much of a surprise. Why? Because your own instincts told you in the dressing room that those skin-tight bell-bottom jeans weren't exactly right. The same concept applies to your career. Sometimes the allure of sexy packaging, whether that's money, prestige, or even a powerful-sounding title, can disguise the realities of a job and tempt you into making a wrong decision.

TALKING ABOUT . . . RECOGNIZING WHAT'S RIGHT FOR YOU

Joan is a successful television sales executive in Los Angeles, California. At thirty-nine, she's already achieved many of her professional dreams. "I've worked for three major companies in my career and almost made a terrible mistake a couple of years ago by going to work for a competitor who offered me an obscene amount of money." Joan is out of the closet in her professional life and told me, "I've always worked for liberal companies, and there have always been lesbians and gay men in high-profile positions. When I was being wooed by company X, I knew they wanted to hire me because of my connections and relationships with station owners, and that wasn't a problem for me. I've worked my butt off to develop those relationships, and they're worth a lot of money. However, I allowed myself to be seduced into overlooking the fact that the company is known not to be very welcoming to women and gays."

After a few weeks of being offered increasingly large salaries, Joan accepted the job. Prior to signing her employment contract, she was invited to a celebration dinner with three highly placed executives, which provided the truth she needed to hear. She rolled her eyes as she said, "By the end of the evening I was so overcome with disgust about the outright lying that went on that night, I knew I couldn't take the job." Joan told me that if the company's leaders felt free to lie about "everything under the sun," including who they are as people, then she couldn't believe in their promises to her. "To begin with, one chief executive is closeted and married. I know he's gay because he hit on a male member of my sales staff at a trade show in Las Vegas. Another one of my hosts that evening is probably the nastiest and most abusive tyrant in television, but he sat there and went on and on about his religious philanthropy. Last but not least, the third man had recently placed a desperate call to a friend of mine about a new job because he thought he was about to be fired. Yet here he sat, going on and on about how successful he was at company X, while the other men praised his talents to the heavens. As it turns out, they were the ones that wanted to fire him! It was the biggest bunch of bullshit I'd seen in a long time, and I knew I couldn't work with such hypocrisy."

Joan said that it was no small coincidence there weren't other women at the table that night. "Unless it's in an area that the male leaders feel is appropriate for women, there isn't much visibility." She added, "A friend of mine who starred in one of their sitcoms put it this way: 'If you don't stand at a urinal to pee, the president of company X will expect you to hold his while he pees!' I knew that when I accepted their offer, but, to be honest, the money blinded me. But the reality of what I was about to get into really hit home. This wasn't the right place for me."

Navigating a road that's right for you is much more about who you are in the world than it is about external motivations such as money, prestige, or power. However, recognizing and valuing your own identity as the source for professional rewards can absolutely result in money, prestige, and power. Often, we think that one benefit precludes another, but when it comes to your career that's simply not true. It's possible to attain all of the sexy benefits associated with a job by first recognizing your value and then listening to and acting upon your own instincts. By doing so you can have it all.

Strengthening Your Professional Instincts

Creating a successful future calls on you to acknowledge your professional instincts, which to a large extent are the result of your life experiences. In this context your instincts aren't a mystical "sixth sense." Rather, they are an asset you can develop and refine in order to successfully navigate a road that's headed in the right direction for you.

There's a good chance that at some point in your professional life you will be tempted by a job that your instincts tell you to avoid. In Joan's case, the temptation came in the form of salary. In other cases, it might be a powerful-sounding title or the promise of a sizable bonus. Paying attention to your professional instincts requires you to tune out the sounds of what I referred to earlier as sexy packaging. If your instincts are telling you to avoid a certain professional situation or workplace environment, in all like-lihood the sexy packaging is not going to make up for the mess you'll find yourself in later. In the majority of circumstances, your professional instincts will lend guidance along your road to success.

EXERCISE **_Developing Your Instincts_**

Set aside fifteen minutes every day for the next two weeks to listen to your professional instincts. Select an issue to focus on that represents a current career goal. For example, your issue may be getting a raise or an extra week's vacation. It may be your goal to come out in the workplace. Feel free to select a new issue each day, or you may decide to concentrate on just one goal per week. Then follow these three steps for each issue to help you identify, assess, and develop your professional instincts.

1. Identify three actions that your instincts are advising you to take and three actions the external world is advising you to take in order to achieve your goal. The external world in this case can include coworkers, friends, partners, or even society in general. List the steps you might take to achieve your goal based on the "advice" of each source.

2. Measure the potential effectiveness of each action. Score each action as likely being effective (3 points), possibly effective (2 points), possibly not effective (1 point), or not effective (0 points) in helping you achieve your goal. In other words, if your issue is to get a raise and the external world advises you to march into your boss's office and demand more money, evaluate the likelihood that this action will result in an increase in salary based on what you know about the environment. If your boss is someone who doesn't respond well to direct and forceful communi-cation, this action would likely be rated "not effective."

3. Evaluate each action based on your scores and determine who provides better advice—you, based on your instincts, or the external world. Write a short sentence or two after each action that describes why you believe that action will or will not likely be effective. In doing so, you will heighten your awareness of your own instinctual effectiveness and be able to extract the best advice from both sources.

TALKING ABOUT . . . GETTING ON THE RIGHT ROAD

Everett, a thirty-three-year-old executive with a major talent agency in Hollywood, California, developed his talents into lucrative career skills because he listened to his professional instincts. As a packaging agent, Everett groups together writers, actors, and producers from the agency's client list as a "package deal" for television networks and motion picture studios. I was confident my interview with Everett was going to be meaningful after reading the letter attached to his survey. "Being a gay man, I knew I needed to pay closer attention to what was right or wrong for me than straight people. I never want to be at the mercy of anyone who doesn't 'approve' of me in order to get ahead in my career." Everett loves his job and told me he has never compromised his primary goal of becoming the most successful agent in the entertainment industry. "I know that 'integrity' isn't the first word that comes to mind when describing agents in Hollywood, but it's the number one reason that I'm going to accomplish my goals. People know they can trust me and I'm not going to bullshit them when it comes to doing business."

Everett cited another source for his success: "I love what I do." At the beginning of his career, however, he found himself on a very different path. "All of the jobs I had in college were with banks, because I didn't think I had the option to follow a career outside the box of my college major, which was finance." After several interviews in his senior year of college for jobs on Wall Street, Everett realized that a career in finance wasn't for him. "I knew I wasn't going to be excited enough to really excel in finance, so instead I went after a creative program development position in the entertainment industry. One of my friend's parents was a programming executive for a television network. Every time I went to her house I couldn't wait to talk to her dad about his job. Working on projects that were seen by millions of people and maybe even influenced lives was exactly what I wanted to do." Even with an inside connection, he found it difficult to break into the field. "Convincing people that I could do the job without any experience was another story. Finally, just to get my foot in the door, I took a position in the finance department at a network since that's where all of my experience had been. It wasn't what I wanted to do, but it was where I wanted to be." By the end of his first year, Everett was working primarily with the business affairs department at the network, helping to negotiate contracts. During that time he also had the opportunity to meet several well-known and respected agents. Two years later he was offered an opportunity to work for a well-known agency, and he has been moving toward his goal ever since. "Recognizing what my talents are and using them in my career has given me the amazing opportunity to mix business with pleasure. When you love what you do and pursue your goals with integrity, there's no better feeling in the world."

Acquiring Specialized Knowledge

Whether you're shy or outgoing, tapping into the professional knowledge of other people will help you connect your professional instincts with the realities of the working world. First, let's reframe the meaning of the word *networking*. Networking is simply about acquiring knowledge to illuminate your professional path, and everyone needs specialized knowledge to succeed. I interviewed several people who were very uncomfortable with even the idea of talking to others about their career goals because it made them feel "needy." But networking is actually a sign of strength and doesn't require you to place yourself in a subordinate position. At its core, networking is simply about being an active listener.

Remember that you're not alone in the working world. Going it alone can produce feelings of separation, loneliness, and frustration. But you're not alone in your desire to achieve your professional dreams, and you will be much more likely to achieve your goals if you seek out the wisdom of others. The real-life knowledge of other members of the gay community is critical in helping you make decisions that allow you to achieve your highest possible level of success.

TALKING ABOUT . . . NETWORKING

Jessie is a thirty-two-year-old architect who told me he had a great deal of difficulty when it came to networking. Looking to make a professional move that would bring him greater responsibility and a higher salary, he attended several professional lunches and seminars in order to learn about new opportunities. "I promised myself that I would come home from each event with ten business cards." When I asked him what he had uncovered from these new connections, he said, "A lot of my contacts didn't return my call."

As we talked, I realized that in his eagerness to develop his network, Jessie was focused on making contacts and not connections. I asked him if he took any notes, mental or written, after these professional events to record any special information that would be helpful when reestablishing the connection later on. "To be honest, I don't remember what some of the people looked like, and I didn't want to refer to something they said when I followed up in case I had the wrong person."

I asked Jessie to concentrate his energies on establishing only three connections per event rather than collecting ten business cards. The goal was to have an honest dialogue with another human being rather than simply acknowledge each other's existence by exchanging business cards. Six months later I followed up with Jessie and he told me that one new connection in particular had been highly successful. "I really tried to establish a rapport with a few of the people I met, and then all of a sudden I felt 'plugged in' to an entirely new group of architects and designers. My initial connection is straight, but several of the people he put me in touch with are gay. It's been a really interesting process seeing how all of these people are interconnected." He told me that he had interviewed with a new firm and was hopeful about the outcome. Two weeks later, as I was reading through my Monday morning email, there was a note from Jessie. The subject heading said it all. It read, "I got the job."

Your Road to Success Is Unique

It's impossible to foresee all of the twists and turns that life holds for us. We simply can't plan for all of the unexpected happenstance that the future may bring. It is, however, possible to equip ourselves with valuable skills like developing and listening to our professional instincts, recognizing how our goals align with the integrity of our employers, and networking.

It's difficult to navigate a road that's headed toward success if you don't believe you have the tools to arrive at your destination. It's even more difficult if you don't even believe you're good enough to be on the road. But when you recognize that you have the ability to apply your talents and skills in a way that brings meaning and fulfillment to your life, you sanction your success. When you acknowledge the value of your unique identity, it's impossible to feel any way other than completely deserving of success. After all, you can't truly measure the value of anything that's one of a kind because there simply isn't anything in existence for comparison. As you move on to the next section and begin to create your own lavender success, remember that you bring unique value to your career because you're unmatched in the world of work.

CREATING YOUR LAVENDER SUCCESS

6

Overcoming Barriers
That Limit Your Success

IN EARLY CIVILIZATIONS, PHYSICAL STRENGTH was the primary requirement
for creating and maintaining success. The weak, or those who appeared to
be weak, were not given the same opportunities to succeed. Today, in our
own society, sexual orientation is still viewed by some as a reason to limit
your professional success. Now here's the good news. You can overcome any
barrier that might block your lavender road to success. When you equip
yourself with knowledge, you can develop a road map that will lead you
over, around, and through the obstacles that might otherwise prevent you
from achieving all of your professional dreams. When you know what the
obstacles are and where they came from, you can defeat them.

Avoiding the Pitfall of Labels

Fifty-four percent of the gay community represented in the survey portion
of my research feel that their sexual orientation has had a negative impact
on their career. It's unquestionable that the professional challenges for the
gay community are much more complex than they are for heterosexuals,
and many career difficulties are indeed rooted in societal influences.

More than 40 percent of survey respondents indicated that they
haven't felt worthy of success since childhood because society told them
that they weren't good enough. Is your family included in that "society"?
Absolutely.

But regardless of where you are right now in your career, identifying early and natural career interests can help you reframe past events that may have resulted in professional barriers.

Beginning in childhood, society impacts the career decision-making process in a powerful way. Contemporary society functions much like early civilizations that limited the success of members who had been defined as weak. A wide range of differences, including sexual orientation, gender identity, and ethnicity, as well as emotional and physical disabilities, are used by some to place people in inferior categories and limit their prospects. If you let them get away with it, you'll limit your ability to succeed. The truth is that your differences make you strong—as a human being, and as a professional.

> *The relationship between sexual orientation and the career planning and development process must be clearly defined in order to create equality in the professional world.*

TALKING ABOUT . . . BEING LABELED

One of the most engaging interviews I had throughout my research was with Olivia, a twenty-four-year-old human resources manager in San Diego, California. Our conversation centered on how she felt society had attempted to limit her success. When we talked about how much, and if, the world had really changed in the last few thousand years, she offered a unique perspective. "The one continuing truth that's allowed oppression to happen since the hunter-gatherers is appearance, which is not related to attractiveness, and completely related to how someone can visually define you as different. I think it's human nature to place people in boxes based on what you see, but it's how you view those boxes that can be destructive. If someone sees me and says, 'Oh, that's Olivia, she's a young, multiracial lesbian,' I don't have a problem with that, unless they think I'm less of a person because I am a young, multiracial lesbian. The problem with labels is that most people use them to put you down."

Traveling Over, Around, and Through Obstacles

There are two major career roadblocks created when you allow yourself to be placed in a category because of your sexual orientation. The first roadblock is created when you accept any type of limitation because you're gay.

When you consent to a work life within the boundaries that others have put there, you provide ongoing support for societal discrimination. The second roadblock occurs simultaneously with the first: your acceptance of others' limitations creates an inner belief that gay people aren't worthy of success. Therefore, you're not worthy of success. This inner belief will permeate all areas of your life and can lead to career decisions that are based entirely on external influences rather than where the focus should always be—on you and your unique identity.

Here's an example of what I mean. Let's say a gay child hears an adult putting negative labels on others because of their sexual orientation. As a result of hearing this, the child begins to believe that anyone who's gay doesn't deserve as much out of life as others. This is the way that gay children learn to limit themselves, and as adults we have to unlearn that type of negative association.

Olivia was completely on target when she said that labels placed on people by society are most often for the purpose of identifying them as inferior. During our interview, she shared with me a very personal account of how this happened in her childhood. "I don't remember exactly how old I was, but I remember my grandfather talking about the guy that cut his hair, and how he thought he was a 'fag.' That's when I became aware that being gay wasn't cool in my grandfather's world. It's also when I started to connect sexual orientation with positive and negative career choices."

In childhood, we begin to form opinions about jobs and the world of work by observing positive and negative associations. For example, Olivia told me that she formed a negative impression about "men who cut hair" based simply on her grandfather's language. For a long time she believed that men who were hairstylists were somehow "bad" because of their profession. Our early opinions about various types of careers are greatly impacted by society because of this association process. And if those early opinions are based on negative associations, they often translate into career obstacles later in life. For a gay child, the potential for negative associations takes on tremendous significance in the career development process, because natural instincts and talents can often be at war with society.

All children begin to form impressions about careers based on a natural association process. For example, if your favorite uncle is an architect, you'll likely form a positive opinion about the field of architecture. The opposite holds true for someone you don't like. If your least favorite uncle is an engineer, you're not going to be excited about going into that field. At the same time that children are forming these early impressions about various careers, they are also beginning to become aware that certain professions are linked to certain genders.

For all children, there may be an innate attraction or talent for a certain career field that isn't supported by traditional patriarchal gender roles assigned by society. It's not unusual for gay children, for whom this issue is especially relevant, to abandon early ideas about interesting careers simply because their families, teachers, or the media have deemed that those careers are not appropriate based on gender. In fact, a negative reaction from society can undermine the early stages of healthy career development, during which all interests should be nurtured and valued.

Society is frightened by little girls who seem interested in traditional "masculine" jobs and of little boys who like things that are considered "feminine."

TALKING ABOUT . . . GENDER-APPROPRIATE JOBS

Craig is a thirty-one-year-old architect in Los Angeles, California. A family member's negative reaction to his innate talent as an artist when he was ten years old is still crystal clear in his mind. "I was always fascinated with my mom's fashion magazines and loved drawing pictures of women's clothes. As far as I knew at ten years old, that was a fine thing to do. But that changed one day when I heard my aunt tell my mom that if she didn't stop me from drawing women's clothes that I'd grow up to be a 'queer fashion worker.' Well, guess what? I was born queer, so take that one off the table right now! But if this kind of bigotry had not served to limit my options, maybe I could have been a famous fashion designer. Who knows?"

When I asked Craig how he felt when he heard his aunt say that his desire to draw would result in his becoming a "queer fashion worker," his remarks were very candid. "I don't think I've ever really talked about this before, but I remember it like it was yesterday. When I heard her say 'queer,' I knew she meant it in a bad way. In fact, beyond bad. I had a basic understanding of what the word meant, even at ten, but hadn't given it a whole lot of thought in terms of my own identity. I mean, I was a little kid for

God's sake." He continued, "I definitely felt like what I had been doing was wrong, which was basically just playing and learning about my own talents. I say that because after that day, I only drew women's clothes when no one was around." Craig told me that he remembers tearing up his drawings into thousands of pieces, and then throwing them in the trash outside so no one would find them. I asked him if he remembered whether or not his

An important step in finding the right job is to identify the constraints placed on you by society as potential roadblocks along your road to success.

mother ever said anything to him that reflected his aunt's homophobic sentiment. "She didn't have to," he said. "She never saw me draw women's clothes again."

The early signs of Craig's artistic and creative abilities were manifested in those drawings of women's clothes. Today, as a successful architect, those same natural gifts have benefited him tremendously. "I found my way into this field because of my artistic talent, but who knows where else I might have gone had I not been stifled. And it wasn't just my aunt. It's all around you when you're growing up gay. There's no doubt in my mind that it's because I'm male that my talents were 'safely' played out in the field of architecture."

EXERCISE **Becoming the Author of Your Success Story**

To write your own success story, begin by recognizing your career dreams without succumbing to the influence of society. When you become the author of your success story, you place primary importance on you, and that includes your early and natural career interests. The purpose of this exercise is to identify what has seemed unattainable up until now. This might be due to the extreme demands of a particular job, like being an astronaut or a heart surgeon, or simply due to society telling you that you can't succeed in that field. Later in this chapter, we're going to take your "unattainable dreams" and change them into new and improved dreams. Why will they be improved? Because these are dreams that you can live out in the real world. Complete the following statements, and don't allow any obstacle from the past to inhibit your responses.

1. In a perfect world, where I could be anything that I want, I would be

_____

2. In the real world, if I had never listened to anyone other than myself, I would be _____

3. If it weren't for _____, I would be a _____

4. Knowing what I know now, I would never have let _____ impact my career decision-making process.

5. _____ was wrong. I have the talent and ability to achieve all of my professional dreams.

Finding Your Perfect Job in the Real World

Knowing what you know today about yourself and the world, it's possible to overcome the obstacles that have limited your success. The past is over, and you can create a new career reality for yourself today. As I've already discussed in the previous chapters, if you make the right career decisions based on who you are, and weigh them against the realities of the world of work, you can realize an amazing level of professional success and, indeed, live your dreams.

In order to bridge these two seemingly disparate worlds—your perfect-world career and the realities of the workplace—we'll use the ingredients of your perfect-world job to create a successful reality. Let's say that your perfect-world job is being the lead dancer with the New York City Ballet. The first step in the process is to identify the "ingredients" of that job, those delicious elements of the career that attracted us in the first place, and transfer them into an achievable reality. For argument's sake, let's also say that you're past the age at which it's necessary to start studying ballet to enter the field, and that you have no formal training. Okay, let's start to discover how to identify those "delicious elements!"

The first thing I would ask if this were your perfect-world job is to articulate what it is about being the lead dancer with the New York City Ballet that excites you. Is it because you long for professional adulation and like being in the spotlight? Are you someone who loves to rehearse and plan prior to performing your work because you expect perfection when it's show time? Perhaps you're attracted to the job because you were born with the ability to creatively interpret complicated material.

Let's say that you're attracted to the job because of the way human emotions are conveyed through body movement. One ingredient you might therefore identify could be your attraction to a job that requires a high degree of thoughtful and interpersonal communication. You can't be a ballet star without teamwork, organization, and planning. If you've ever seen dancers being lifted into the air, you know that their success depends on the expertise of their colleagues. Therefore, being the lead dancer with the New York City ballet isn't a job that you do in isolation. The plans that

You have the ability to transfer the elements of a perfect-world job into professional opportunities that you can begin to pursue today.

go into a ballet production are intricate, and someone who likes to fly by the seat of their pants isn't going to find success in a job that requires carefully choreographed moves.

These ingredients are important in many career fields, and you don't have to give any of them up when you transfer what you're attracted to in a perfect-world job into an achievable reality. When you take your ingredients with you, you're creating a professional bridge between the two worlds, and your resulting success will be remarkable.

To build on the work you did in the previous exercise, make a list of the ingredients that are necessary for your perfect job. Don't allow traditional gender roles to influence your list. Remember, the ingredients aren't masculine or feminine, gay or straight. They attract you because of who you are as a whole person, and that includes your sexual orientation and innate talents. Denying your ideal because you think it's traditionally unacceptable is the professional equivalent of turning your back on success. When you complete your list, put it in a prominent place and live with your "delicious elements." Make yourself aware of how rich life can be when you're inviting your successful ingredients into your world.

Discovering Lost Career Dreams

When discussing the topic of professional barriers and limits, I found that sometimes when career dreams are lost, either to societal influences or to homophobia, many gay people have difficulty defining themselves as successful—even when society itself would characterize them as wildly successful.

For many gay people who have become prosperous and respected, there's an inescapable feeling that nothing can ever equal their lost dreams.

It's interesting to note that the people who feel this way usually did not transfer significant ingredients from their "lost" careers to their current professional lives.

TALKING ABOUT . . . LOST DREAMS

Luke is a thirty-three-year-old corporate attorney in San Francisco with a healthy income and impressive work history that would rival that of a seasoned legal veteran. Along with his survey, he wrote an articulate letter about how he had to make a choice between his ideal job and freedom. "Being an attorney was never part of my plan. In fact, it wasn't even on my radar screen." Since childhood, Luke has been passionate about sports. "I remember going to Dodger Stadium and dreaming about being inducted into the Baseball Hall of Fame." But in his junior year of high school, something happened to change his mind about pursuing a career as a baseball player. "I always knew it, but I finally owned up, to myself at least, that I am gay."

Success isn't about what others see, it's about what we know.

He told me, "I never came out or acted on my attraction for other guys in high school, so definitely no one on my baseball team, or at school, knew I was gay. On the field, I'd hear my teammates, and even the coach, call a player he thought wasn't giving 100 percent 'faggot,' and then deliberately torment anyone they thought might actually be gay. At the time, I went along with it and did the same thing, because I was terrified of what would happen otherwise. But it didn't feel right. Every time I called somebody 'faggot,' it was like beating myself up. It made me feel like shit." College scouts, who were crisscrossing the country to recruit star baseball players for their respective university teams, had already been knocking at his door. "I know I could've got a great scholarship, and who knows what could have happened beyond college. But it was too much of a sacrifice to go along with the lie." In his senior year, Luke remained closeted and the star of his baseball team. He also stopped participating in all other school activities. "I just kept to myself so I could avoid the whole situation." Luke told me that it was his own social withdrawal as a high school senior that finally made him decide that a career in sports wasn't going to be available to him on his terms. "I didn't want to live that way." The summer before he entered college, Luke came out of the closet and has never regretted his decision. "I've had incredible support from my family, and choosing my own freedom over a career in sports was the right thing to do." Then, after a long pause, he added, "But I wouldn't say that I'm successful, even though I have all the trappings of what most people call success. Every time I win a case, get a promotion, or win an award, I go to bed that night thinking about what might have been if the sports world wasn't so damned homophobic."

Conquering the Closet

In order to truly achieve success, you need to be truthful with yourself, your employer, and society. Being truthful with yourself means that you embrace your sexual orientation and believe that you are equal in value to the rest of the human population. If you're gay, then being gay is a natural state of being for you.

In section one we talked about many of the realities—positive and negative—that impact your career when you're in the closet. At this point in the book, as you begin the process of selecting, finding, and landing your perfect job, it's important to take another look at how being gay and being out can actually enhance your professional value.

Gene Falk, senior vice president of Showtime Networks, is also responsible for spearheading the development of the company's new gay cable network. He shared his thoughts with me on the subject of how being out at work can actually enhance your career. "Coming out and staying out changes your life. It changes the way you think about your career. In terms of how your sexual orientation can actually be a benefit, there are two ways to look at it. Specific gay-related projects have come my way because I've placed myself in an environment that values what I bring to the table as a gay man. In my industry, for example, it's recognized that the gay audience is very valuable. Therefore, I've gained additional recognition through opportunities that came about because of my sexual orientation." Outside work, Gene has been successfully involved with nonprofits and philanthropic work, which brings into play the second way being out in your career can make a positive impact. "Getting involved in organizations like GLAAD, for example, broadens your understanding about the human condition. Not only did serving

Being out of the closet will put you on a path where barriers are replaced with opportunities.

on the board of GLAAD for several years provide me with new life experiences that ultimately enhanced my job performance, but involvement also gave me positive visibility. As a result, I became more valuable as a professional in my field."

Rendering Your Barriers Powerless

While I was knee-deep in research materials on a Sunday afternoon, my partner, Kirwan, convinced me to take a break and go to an action movie. Although I'm not usually a fan of the genre, it sounded like it would be thoroughly entertaining. As it turned out, the plot had a great deal of relevance to the work I left at home! In the movie, which of course had a hero and a bad guy, the bad guy changed the basic structure of his DNA, transforming himself into an entirely new person, inside and out. Now, this new person was completely unrecognizable to the hero, even after they had met face to face on several occasions. So, for a substantial part of the movie, the hero was unable to defeat his nemesis because the hero couldn't recognize the barriers he needed to overcome. Of course, once the hero figured it out, his nemesis had a limited amount of time left to live.

Overcoming barriers that limit your professional success requires recognizing those segments of society that create and sustain homophobia.

Although I don't advise using the same high-tech tactics applied in the movie to overcome societal barriers to your career, the same dynamic does, in fact, hold true as you travel your lavender road to success. Recognizing your "nemesis," including those negative societal influences that create obstacles in your career, empowers you to move swiftly toward your professional goals.

Some barriers may only exist in the past, and others may exist in the present. Either way, your goal is to identify them and render them powerless over your life. When that occurs, you'll find that you're refocused on what's really important—you and a professional future with unlimited success.

● ● ●

One definition of the word *community* is a group of people that come together to share experiences. This book attempts to create a community in which everyone can achieve their career goals. Believing in your own innate value based on who you are as an individual—including being gay—will always be your primary career resource. But remember that you're not alone. There's a strong and supportive community across the country and the world that believes in you. Being gay is not a weakness and it is not a reason to limit your success. You *can* overcome barriers— and when you believe in your right to succeed as yourself there's no limit to what you can achieve.

Empowering
Yourself to Achieve

RECENTLY I MET MY BEST FRIEND and her two young daughters for lunch. When I arrived at the restaurant, they were just walking in after a visit to the toy store next door. Both girls couldn't wait to show me their new purchases and were more than ready to tear open the boxes on the spot. Since each of the toys required assembly, my friend asked them to wait until they got home to put them together so they could use the right kind of tools. Now, if you've been around any five- and seven-year-olds recently, you'll know that her idea didn't go over very well. Finally, after tireless negotiation, my friend gave up and let her daughters open their toys and start putting them together. Like most of us when we want something right now, the girls thought they could get to the "good stuff" by starting in the middle of the assembly process rather than starting at the beginning and using the appropriate tools. What happened next isn't surprising. The first toy broke while using a house key instead of the required screwdriver, and the second toy wouldn't work because two important pieces were put in upside down.

Conducting a successful job search is exactly like putting a child's toy together. You need to assemble all of the pieces in the right order if you want the result to be a fully functioning product. There's nothing wrong with wanting to realize all of your professional dreams right now, but short-circuiting the process won't get you there any faster. In fact, it causes delays and frustrations. For the gay community, the first tool required for putting together a successful job search is feeling good about yourself and who you are in the world. When you start on a positive and affirming note, you'll grant yourself the authority to achieve and succeed—at every point in your career.

Starting on the Right Path

When I first meet clients who are already in the process of looking for a job, I always ask the same question: "What was the first thing you did when you decided to find a new job?" Ninety percent of the time I get the same response, "I looked at job listings." For members of the gay community, immediately reading job listings before you address how you feel about you can lead to an undesirable outcome. Feeling good about who you are in the world is a powerful career tool that's too often overlooked.

If you begin your job search by looking at job listings, you are placing more importance on the job than you are on yourself.

Keep in mind that a job can't be successful, only you can. Once I hear that clients have "started in the middle" by going immediately to the job listings, the first thing I do is open up a dialogue to determine how they feel about themselves and being gay. Right now, ask yourself this question: "Do I believe I'm capable and deserving of success?" Assess where you stand with you. The following exercise is designed to help you gain a deeper understanding about how your feelings toward your sexual orientation can impact the way you look for a job.

EXERCISE **Where Do I Stand with Me?**

Feeling good about yourself is the bedrock of a successful job search. If you jump in feet first, before you address where you stand with you, you'll risk placing barriers between yourself and your career goals. Give yourself the freedom to honestly answer these three questions. Your answers must be "yes" or "no." There should be no answers in the middle for this particular exercise. Expand each answer with a two- to three-sentence explanation about why you feel this way.

1. Do I worry that I won't be hired for a good job because of workplace homophobia?

2. Do I worry that an employer will think I'm too feminine, too masculine, or too "gay" to be hired?

3. Do I wish I were straight?

If you answered yes to any of these questions, then you're not completely onboard with the belief that you are okay just the way you are. This fact may be difficult to admit, but being aware of how you feel about yourself and being gay is critical to a successful job search. As you move forward in this chapter, you'll find out how others in the gay community have turned negative feelings into positive ones.

Learning to Appreciate Yourself

How many times have you heard the following statement, "Of course sexual orientation isn't a choice. Why would anyone choose such a difficult life?"? More often than not, the intention behind this statement is likely honorable. Supporters, allies, and even members of our own community routinely deliver this message as a way to advocate for equal gay rights. However, inherent in this statement is the implication that being gay is second-best. Authentic appreciation for yourself requires some hard work. If you grow up hearing that being gay is undesirable, you must, as an adult, break away from those negative influences and create the truthful recognition that being gay is just as valuable as being straight. When you start to understand just how valuable you are in the world, you'll begin to appreciate yourself and your professional capabilities in ways you've never experienced.

TALKING ABOUT . . . FEELING WORTHY OF SUCCESS

When I started to receive responses to my initial survey I was amazed at how many people sent along detailed letters offering to share their personal career experiences. Nearly 70 percent of the survey respondents made themselves available for one-on-one interviews. When I received Michael's survey, not only did he enclose three complete pages of detail, but he also included a moving personal letter asking me to share his story. He felt his experiences would be particularly important to young gay people still in college who may be struggling with their own identity. Once we spoke on the phone, I knew the exact place in the book where his wisdom about the importance of feeling worthy of success would shine through.

Michael's story is extremely important because it leaves no doubt that feeling good about being gay has a direct and favorable impact on your career. A thirty-eight-year-old gay Latino, Michael didn't come out until he was thirty-one. "It's all about believing that gay is as good as straight," he told me. "When I was hiding, I always hated going to work. Even looking for a job made me nauseous. Trying to convince everyone that I was straight because of 'cultural machismo' brought about a set of problems that will unfortunately never end." Since Michael found out he was HIV-positive at age thirty, he has found professional help to protect both his physical and emotional well-being. Even under what he describes as "extremely stressful circumstances" relative to the maintenance of his physical health, coming out and getting to the place where he believed that gay is okay had a dramatic and favorable impact on his professional life. "When I was forced to confront my sexuality because of my illness— it sounds crazy, but my career started to take off for the first time." I asked him why he felt coming out of the closet made such a difference in his professional life. "Because it meant that, finally, I could be myself, and that has translated into liking myself. When you're hiding," he told me, "you feel shame."

Since our first conversation, I've had the opportunity to speak with Michael many times about reaching his professional goal of becoming director of graphic arts with his current employer, a major regional advertising agency. Since coming out, not only has he placed himself within an inclusive and gay-friendly workplace environment, but he's also received two promotions in the last two years and is only one step away from realizing his goal. I asked him if he felt there was a difference in the way he pursued a position now that he's out of the closet. "Now I know I can aim as high as I can dream. The lie that's put into your head by others, and that you have to reject, is that being gay is the same as being last in line. Once I found the strength to realize that being gay is just as valuable as being straight, not only could I see the point where I wanted to go in my career, but I could even see beyond it."

Michael's ultimate realization of his own value is based on three behaviors:

- Accepting and integrating his sexual orientation into his unique identity

- Actively finding support and encouragement through a network that believed in him

- Identifying a professional destination that's worthy of a valuable person, and then stepping out onto the road headed toward that success

And you can do it too.

Celebrating Your Own Importance

One of the most practical and effective approaches I've used with clients to create a strong sense of appreciation for who they are in the world, and therefore the sense that they are empowered to achieve all of their career goals, is to look at the process as if they were starting their own business. A practical analogy like this simply makes it easier to develop and implement the steps that ultimately lead to self-confidence, optimism about the future, and authority over your own career. What's the product going to be in your new business? Self-appreciation.

Putting together a winning job search requires a foundation of self-appreciation. Without it, you'll never be focused on the most important part of your lavender road to success—you. Begin by becoming an observer of your own importance and value. Don't worry: it's not about complicated introspection, but simply about understanding that you already have the basic requirements for success. In other words, you already have what it takes! This four-step, easy-to-use "business plan" approach will get you started in the right direction.

1. **Declare your mission.** All successful businesses start with a mission statement to provide a sense of purpose and direction. Read your following mission statement aloud: "My mission is to discover and better understand my own unique importance and value as a gay person in the professional world."

2. **Establish your factory.** In order to build your product of self-appreciation, you'll need a high-quality and gay-friendly workforce! Identify three or four people (or groups) who will become your *network of positive reinforcement.* Your network can be made up of friends, family, adopted family, support groups, or professional organizations that empower you to feel important and valuable. It's irrelevant whether

members of your network are gay or straight, as long as each person (or group) makes no negative value judgments about your sexual orientation. Your network members should:

- Be completely supportive of the gay community

- Demonstrate the ability to listen and be available

- Have your best interest at heart, with no hidden agenda

- Be able to tell you the truth in a positive way, even if you don't want to hear it

- Provide positive reinforcement that who you are is important and valuable, and what you want to accomplish in the world of work is worthy of an important and valuable person

3. **Build your product.** Invite the potential members of your network to become part of your job search process. Let them know that you'd like their partnership in keeping you focused on your importance and value. Remember, this particular network isn't about job leads or professional connections, but simply about being focused on why you deserve to be appreciated. Does that include an appreciation for being gay? Yes, it's a requirement. Your sexual orientation is, after all, part of who you are, and therefore part of what's valuable in the makeup of your unique identity. So, whether the members of your network reinforce your specific talents and skills or just acknowledge that you make their lives better because you're you, they will remind you on a regular basis that you deserve to be successful.

4. **Review your productivity.** As you interact with members of your network on an ongoing basis, be sure to chronicle your experiences. Make a list that highlights the reasons why you're appreciated. Reviewing your list on a regular basis will anchor your foundation of self-appreciation.

● ● ●

It's important to manage your network in a way that continues to support your mission statement. If some members of your network aren't providing you the right kind of support, replace them. It doesn't mean that they don't care about you or don't believe you're talented. All it means is that, in this context, they aren't helping you to manufacture your product of self-appreciation. Trust your instincts. Don't forget that as a member of the gay community, feeling good about yourself is always going to be connected to feeling good about your sexual orientation, so your process will benefit when you quickly disengage from any part of your network that doesn't reinforce this truth. The rule of thumb is that if you feel encouraged and good about yourself after any interaction, then you should keep the relationship in your network, and even spend time to nurture that particular connection. Focus on what works for you.

Defeating the Naysayers

The importance of learning from the wisdom of others is something I'm reminded of daily. As often as we can arrange it, I get together with a good friend of mine at the university for a "theme lunch." In keeping with the tradition we've established, we email back and forth a few days ahead and agree on a topic to discuss over lunch. We've discussed such diverse topics as presidential elections, university politics, and the latest Hollywood divorce. My friend's name is Sally, and she's a thirty-seven-year-old straight African-American woman who has succeeded professionally, often in the face of great adversity, with her humor and compassion for others intact. We called one of our lunches "Defeating the Naysayers," and it turned out to be extremely relevant to this chapter. Sally's wisdom about reclaiming her authority to assign value to her own individuality empowered her to achieve her professional dreams.

That day over lunch, she told me that when she was eighteen and starting college at USC almost twenty years ago, she didn't think that being accepted would be a struggle. "I thought this was a sophisticated urban campus, and I wouldn't have any difficulty because of my race or gender. But during my very first week, I found out how wrong I'd been in that mind-set. I also learned that a lot of the so-called 'great thinkers' who were supposed to teach and encourage me weren't so brilliant when it came to diversity and equal access for all students. Right away, I figured out that some professors and administrators would have preferred that I just go away." In her freshman and sophomore years, Sally often considered changing her major from economics to a field of study that the "great thinkers" deemed more appropriate for a woman of color, such as education or social work. "Because I was studying a subject that was dominated by white males, I was facing two forms of opposition, one because I'm black, and the other because I'm a woman."

Sally and I both agree that the African-American and gay communities have the shared experience of being on the receiving end of what can often be blind hatred, just because of our own identities. Sally, however, pointed out one major difference between the two communities—she couldn't hide who she was even if she wanted to.

Sitting in the center of campus during our lunch, she looked around, reflecting on the environment she encountered nearly twenty years ago. "I think the big difference between your path and mine is that when I was here as a student, I was forced to figure out how to succeed in the world as myself. Long before I ever thought about succeeding in my career, I learned how to succeed as a student. And that meant learning to appreciate my difference, which is also my strength." Then she said something that's as true today as it was then. "But gay, straight, black, white, or in-between, the very reason anyone feels the need to pretend in the first place is because they're buying into the bullshit that says there's something wrong with them. If I would have accepted the oppression and mind-set of all those professors and administrators who didn't want me in class or even on this campus, I wouldn't be here and be successful today."

Appreciation for yourself opens the door to success.

As a gay person, when you pretend to be straight, you delay your discovery of your unique importance and strengths. I asked Sally how she overcame the negative influences of those professors and administrators. She told me, "The most important thing I did for myself after a year and a half of struggling was to accept the fact that all of those 'great thinkers' who hated me because of my skin color and gender weren't such great thinkers after all. You can analyze it for days, but what it comes down to is fear—not on my part, but theirs. They were afraid of losing some of their own power if it turned out that I could do what they do. Look, the only way to get to the place in your head where you can appreciate yourself for how great you really are is to find a strong support system of people who believe in you and are willing to recognize that your difference is your strength." Sally's support system came in the form of one remarkable African-American woman who was working as a teaching assistant in one of her classes while completing her doctorate degree. "With the help of only one woman, I realized that I had the ability to succeed and, more important, the authority to succeed. Never let anyone tell you that you can't or you shouldn't because of your color, gender, sexual orientation, or any other part of what makes you strong. Sometimes it's hard to see that in yourself. We all need a little help to see our own amazing qualities."

Gaining Confidence by Assigning Value to Your Own Identity

Being on the job market can sometimes feel like you're continually seeking the approval of strangers. Allowing others to measure your personal and professional qualities rather than measuring them yourself lets others to determine the value of your unique identity. Gay people face discrimination based on components of their identity, so it's critical to your pursuit of success to reject any negative value that might be imposed on you by others.

While reading through some of the first surveys I received in my research, I came across a note written by the oldest participant in the study, a gay man of eighty. Stapled to his survey was a note that said, "If you let the world tell you what you should be, you'll never know what you are capable of being." The wisdom in that note brought my "Defeating the Naysayers" lunch with Sally full circle. True professional value is something that can only be self-defined. Plain and simple.

We're all products of our own histories. At this very point in time, the combination of biology and environment has made you who you are. This mixture includes where you came from, who raised you, where you went to school, who your friends have been, and all of the events—good and bad—that have happened along the way. For the gay community, the negative influences that originate in the external world and pertain to your sexual orientation can erode confidence in your own unique identity.

TALKING ABOUT . . . CONFIDENCE

Sam, a thirty-three-year-old pharmacist in Berkeley, California, remembers being praised at home for being an A student and ridiculed at school for being gay. "Sometimes it was like living in two dimensions. Beginning in the first grade, I was called names at school. In the beginning, it was 'sissy-boy' or 'girly-boy.' By the fifth grade, it was 'queer' and 'faggot' and worse. When you're told on a daily basis that you're 'wrong' as a human being, it affects you. It makes you feel like you're less deserving of anything good because you're not the same as everyone else."

Sam feels that he was luckier than a lot of gay kids because, as a young child, his maternal grandmother lived with his family, and she was a positive influence. As a young woman Sam's grandmother had been a professional dancer, and after getting married at twenty-five, she moved to San Francisco and opened up a dancing school. "She always had lots of gay friends from her dancing career around her, and she was probably the most generous and open-minded person that's ever lived." Then he surprised me by his candor. "She's also the reason why I didn't commit suicide as a teenager." Sam told me that the most important conversation in his life to date happened after a brutal experience in the second grade. "I was chased home by three kids who were calling me 'gay boy' while they pelted me with rocks. When I finally got inside our house and told my grandmother what happened, she sat me down and told me she was going to let me in on a special truth. Holding my hand and looking straight into my eyes, she said that being gay was a gift that God only gave to very special people. She said that the boys who chased me home didn't know that only very special people were given the chance to be gay, because they simply weren't special enough to know! That was an amazing moment in my life." It turned out that it was also the first part of his grandmother's mission to teach Sam that he had the power to define his own value.

When you take control of assigning your own value, you empower yourself to triumph in all phases of the job search process.

Not too long after that memorable day, Sam's grandmother went to live with another daughter on the opposite coast. Several years later, she returned to live out the end of her life with Sam's family. "When she moved back in with us, things had gotten really bad for me again, and I thought about suicide on a regular basis. My grandmother, who was then very ill, knew that I was at my breaking point." Sam's voice started to choke up as he continued to share his story. "Somehow she found the strength to make me believe, once again, that I was special. I'm convinced to this day that in her heart, she knew I wasn't going to make it without her. That's why she came back to live with us. She had enough financial resources to go anywhere she wanted, but I truly believe she wanted to make sure I'd be okay before she left this earth." He took a deep breath and told me, "The reason I'm here and successful today is because of her love and belief in me. She taught me to define my own goodness, and I've never let her memory down. I use her wisdom every day of my life to feel good about being one of the special people in the world."

Authorizing Yourself to Advance

If you take a close look at the CEOs and presidents at some of the top businesses around the country, you'll quickly discover that the professional path each has taken is as varied as the working world itself. This reality is both inspiring and encouraging because it means that there's a unique road to success for everyone. Even though their paths are varied, each of these leaders likely shared a common experience—they all felt they had the authority to achieve their current level of professional success.

Where does the gay community fit into this paradigm? Most of the gay people who are out of the closet and define themselves as successful that I interviewed could identify a point along their varied career paths where they discovered or reclaimed their own personal value. In fact, one of the major factors that has contributed to their success is feeling good about who they are in the world. This factor has acted as a professional propeller, advancing them beyond their original career goals. All of these successful gay people believe they are authorized to achieve. Who gave them that authority? They did, and you can give yourself the same authorization.

TALKING ABOUT . . . ASSIGNING YOURSELF VALUE

Ted is a forty-one-year-old real estate broker in Hermosa Beach, California, who at the age of twenty-one, stuck his toe into the out-of-the-closet waters by telling some close friends about being attracted to other men. "One night after a party we were sitting around talking about our families, our fears, and the whole 'what am I going to do with my life' thing. Why I suddenly decided to get honest with them that night, at a conservative school in conservative Texas, is beyond me." He paused, then said, "Actually, I do know. It's because I really needed to talk about it, and I thought these people cared about me." Instead of making him feel better, it kicked off a miserable year and a half of his life. He told me, "Even before I went home that night, I was already an outcast. In fact it was worse than being an outcast—it was like I had committed the most heinous crime imaginable."

Struggling to graduate under extremely difficult and, on two occasions, violent circumstances, Ted left his home state of Texas for Southern California and graduate school immediately after his last final as a college senior. "I didn't even stay for the ceremony. I needed to get as far away from everyone and everything in my world as quickly as possible." Because he didn't feel he could talk to his family about what was going on at school, he had absolutely no emotional support in his life. "When I look back at all I went through, I'm amazed that I survived."

We are all products of our past, and it's human nature to avoid putting your hand on that hot stove for the second time. For Ted, the negative reaction he experienced in college convinced him to go as far back into the closet as possible. "Even though I went to graduate school in Los Angeles, and it was light-years ahead of Texas in terms of being gay-friendly, I made the decision to never risk the possibility of going through anything like that again." After he earned his MBA, Ted entered the real estate sales field and jumped from office to office along the California coast. "I never really accomplished anything when I changed jobs, but that wasn't my goal. Each new position was pretty much a lateral move, and I never stayed long enough to make many friends. Quite honestly, I didn't want to be in a position to care about people, because if they rejected me, I'd be right back in the same place I was in Texas."

Until a few years ago, Ted wouldn't have had that insight to share. "I'd still be hopping from job to job and running away if I hadn't stumbled into a life-changing employment situation." The catalyst that ultimately changed Ted's life at thirty-three came in the unexpected form of a successful gay boss who was proud to be out of the closet. "It was like everything I had based my life on since college was wrong. At first, I didn't want to deal with it, having a boss who wasn't just gay, but totally out of the closet. He was also sort of a macho man, which totally blew away any stereotypes I had in my head." After six months of watching from the sidelines, Ted realized that everything he thought was true about being gay was a lie. "I had believed all of my friends back in college that being gay was something that I should be ashamed of and should hide. For a long time, I let other people tell me about myself, instead of me telling them about who I am."

EXERCISE **Authorizing Yourself to Be Successful**

1. List any event or time in your life when you allowed the words of others to negatively impact how you feel about yourself. For example, many people I interviewed were verbally harassed as children and teenagers. In Sam's case, he was called names on his way home from school. For others, the experience was less direct. You may recall how Craig overheard his aunt use the word *queer* in a negative way. Still others have experienced verbal harassment as adults on the job.

2. Next to each occurrence on your list, write down how the words used by other people made you feel at the time. Did you feel like running away? Were you angry? Did you feel "less-than" or maybe even afraid?

3. The same ignorance and fear that generated those words also attached a negative meaning to them. Therefore, I'd like you to redefine the words themselves by attaching a new, positive meaning. You may recall the wisdom of Sam's grandmother, who told Sam that *gay* really means "special."

   As an educated and fully enlightened adult, you have the authority to redefine these words. Other examples of new, positive meanings could be "unique," "rare," "loving," "creative," and so on. Reframe the way you see yourself from this point forward by getting rid of past negative influences that were born out of ignorance and fear.

Creating Success through Self-Esteem

Finding success and professional fulfillment early in your career is directly connected to coming out and feeling good about your sexual orientation at an early age. Eighty-five percent of the people in my study under the age of thirty who are out of the closet at work and describe themselves as successful came to terms with their sexuality prior to launching their careers. This finding supports what Sally, Michael, Sam, and Ted each experienced under very different circumstances at different times in their lives. When you take over the job of defining who you are and how much value your unique identity actually provides, you will be empowered to realize and sustain your highest possible level of professional success.

TALKING ABOUT . . . FINDING SUCCESS

Holly is a twenty-five-year-old account executive in New York who has been out of the closet since she was fourteen. She approaches the process of looking for a job using specific criteria that she says are "rooted in my love for me." Not only has Holly quickly climbed the ladder at a well-known advertising firm, she's also the perfect example of how coming to terms with your sexual orientation at an early age can give you the kind of self-esteem that leads to immediate success in the workplace. "I know I'm lucky because I've always had the support of my family. A lot of my lesbian and gay male friends weren't as lucky, and it was a real struggle for them. The good news is that fortunately, your biological family isn't your only family. There's a whole world out there of incredible people who are smart enough to love you for who you are. The bottom line is that however you can get to the place in your soul where you actually embrace your gayness, do it. Before you can find success at work, you have to believe you're successful as a human being."

TALKING ABOUT . . . AUTHORING YOUR DREAMS

Like many people in the gay community, Gwen believed that she would be prevented from being successful because of her sexual orientation. "I didn't think I could ever become an attorney, even though I've always dreamed about standing in front of a jury and arguing cases. The first time I watched *L.A. Law* as a kid, I said to myself, 'This is what I want to do!' But at the same time, I started to believe that being gay meant I had no right to do what I wanted to do." When I asked Gwen why she linked her sexual orientation with the feeling that she didn't have the "right" to become an attorney, she immediately told me that it was because in high school, she was ostracized as "the dyke."

Gwen told me that after being harassed on a continual basis, "It's easy to start believing that hate has validity. In the small Midwestern town with no diversity where I came from, being gay was about as low on the social ladder as you could get. I was told I was going to hell on a daily basis, and it wasn't just other kids. It was teachers and even parents of other kids in the neighborhood. So it didn't take long for me to start feeling like I didn't have a future."

Gwen's experience since leaving her hometown and enrolling in what she likes to call "a big city college" is a lesson on how to overcome negative influences and achieve success. Away from home for the first time, she found support through a large gay student community. "One of my friends knew I wanted to be an attorney and introduced me to a law professor who happened to be a lesbian. Seeing is believing for me. After meeting this woman and realizing that successful lesbian attorneys really do exist, I started to think that maybe I could do it too."

That was more than seven years ago and now, at twenty-eight, Gwen has completed law school, has passed the bar, and is a practicing attorney. "Sometimes I think about where I was in high school and wonder if there's another gay kid back there being told, 'You can't do anything in life, because you're a piece of shit.'" I asked her what she'd like to say to those gay kids who may be walking in the same shoes she wore in high school. Her response was so quick that I knew it was something she'd thought about many times. "I'd say that you are good enough and cool enough to be whatever you want to be. I'd say that you are good enough and cool enough to have people love and care about you. Finally, I'd tell them that being gay isn't about what other people say you are, so don't let anyone tell you that you're not perfect just the way you are today."

● ● ●

The role society plays in your career goes beyond the job selection process and impacts the way you work. In order to overcome all types of professional limitations, you must believe that who you are brings unique value to your job performance—and your sexual orientation is part of who you are. If you're employed by a gay-friendly organization that provides you with an equal chance to succeed, you should have no need to edit your behavior in order to achieve your professional goals. Your ideas for improving an organization, the types of assignments you undertake, and your actual approach to work should have no masculine or feminine requirements or boundaries. Your success will ultimately be based on your unique identity, which simply means that who you are is the right way to be.

8

Overcoming Homophobia in the Workplace

AT AN INTERNATIONAL CONFERENCE on behavioral learning, a well-known scholar told all of us in the audience that, "The evolution of almost all social issues in our society can be tracked by studying television guides over the last fifty years." Needless to say, many in the audience of researchers, writers, and professors were up in arms. An Ivy League professor sitting next to me shifted in his seat and said, "That's outrageous. You can't reduce the work of sociologists to the log lines of sitcoms and courtroom dramas!"

The speaker was fully aware that he hit a raw nerve, undoubtedly on purpose. From the stage, he smiled politely and suggested that anyone who disagreed should take a look at the programs from television's golden age and compare them with this week's prime-time lineup. Taking him up on his challenge, I began to think about his statement in terms of gay-related content.

A few weeks after the conference, the idea of television documenting the evolution of society reoccurred to me in my living room. Using my remote control as a time travel device, I was able to span a period of fifty years, from 1950s reruns on Nick at Night, to more modern but still homophobic programs of the 1970s, to where we are today, with the latest episode of Showtime's *Queer as Folk*.

Although today's political, legal, and cultural landscapes make it much easier to find a workplace where you can be comfortably out of the closet, in certain parts of the country the level of homophobia remains much the same as it was when television overwhelmed us with heterosexist images. But even though homophobia is still alive and well in far too many living and working environments across the country, you can absolutely make career choices that will remove this monster from your life. Although these choices aren't always easy to make, especially because it may mean moving to a new city, living your daily professional life with anxiety and fear isn't living. Homophobia will prevent you from achieving your highest possible level of success. In this chapter we're going to examine different types of homophobia that exist in the workplace, meet people who have experienced mistreatment and abuse in these environments, and then determine the level at which you may be affected in your own career. My goal is for you to recognize homophobia in the world of work in order to become empowered to leave it behind.

There are no professional advantages to be gained when you submit to the prejudices of others.

Making Career Decisions That Provide Equal Opportunity

One of the most encouraging trends that emerged from my research is that younger members of the gay community are actively seeking a welcoming and inclusive workplace. For example, in my research 97 percent of gay people thirty-five and under said it was important to have a gay-friendly boss. Mitch, a thirty-year-old financial analyst in Los Angeles, mirrors the attitude expressed by his peers. "Don't forget that you are interviewing the company, too. See if this is a gay-friendly place for you to work that fits with your belief system." He told me, "My gay friends work in all kinds of companies where being gay isn't detrimental to their careers, but we are all living and working in large, diverse cities. At the risk of sounding overly optimistic, you can find gay-friendly employment options in most industries, but not necessarily in all places." I asked Mitch what he felt made the difference for gay people in larger cities. "I believe the biggest contributing factor that makes one location more gay-friendly than another is the educational background of the people who live there and who run the city. And it's the same dynamic within a company. If the people who work there and run the company are educated and thinking people who live in today's world, then you'll probably find a gay-friendly employer that welcomes diversity. A few people in my graduating class started with companies in really unfriendly locations, and they had terrible experiences."

Mitch's assessment that a workplace is more likely to be gay-friendly because of education level may at first sound a bit elitist, but logic dictates that the personality of a workplace environment and its geographic location can absolutely be influenced by demographics. Remember Sheila and Anne, partners living in Atlanta that you met in chapter 4? Sheila is free to be out of the closet at work, and Anne is not. The area immediately surrounding Sheila's workplace, metro Atlanta, has a higher percentage of college graduates per capita, at 36.7 percent, than the city where Anne works, where it is only 22.4 percent. The reason this makes a difference has much less to do with the effects of acquiring knowledge in a classroom than with the role higher education plays in offering opportunities to interact with a diverse group of people. The bottom line is that those who don't attend institutions of higher learning are much less likely to be exposed to diversity. Without exposure, there's no opportunity to gain a personal appreciation for people with different ethnic backgrounds, political or religious affiliations, or sexual orientations.

Educational background is also related to economics. The lack of a college education generally leads to fewer opportunities and lower salaries, which can pave the way for feelings of anger and despair. Often the easiest way for people without hope to regain a sense of power is to harm those who are different, particularly if they belong to a minority demographic group.

TALKING ABOUT . . . HOMOPHOBIC REGIONS

Brett is a thirty-eight-year-old regional marketing executive in Los Angeles who regularly visits his employer's numerous retail sites in Southern California. Although he works for an inclusive and gay-friendly organization, his position requires extensive client interaction outside corporate headquarters. "My boss is a with-it guy who embraces diversity, and the company even has domestic partner benefits. In fact, my partner and I go out to dinner with my boss and his wife on a regular basis." Despite these ideal circumstances, however, Brett told me about a recent and completely unexpected experience with work-related homophobia that occurred when he was out in the field at a retail store in a somewhat rural area just outside

Los Angeles. "After I visited the store, I attended a Chamber of Commerce meeting with that city's mayor and community leaders to discuss retail and business activity in the region. These meetings are part of my job, and I've been to a lot of them. But this was the first one in that city. The next day, my boss came into my office and was fuming—not at me, at the mayor. He said that the mayor had called him and asked him why he had a 'gay guy' representing the company at 'his meeting.' He told my boss that I didn't fit in with the family-type environment they promoted in their city and he wanted my boss to send someone that was 'normal' next time. Thank God my boss and the company are gay-friendly or I could've lost my job." Brett said that even though he was completely supported by his employer, it still felt like he'd been kicked in the stomach. I couldn't believe anyone that was an elected official in Southern California, even in a sleepy little town like that, could be so ignorant."

Living in a city like Los Angeles, where acceptance and diversity are part of the region's personality, it's easy to forget that only fifty miles away a pocket culture of homophobia can exist. What's apparent is that in these areas any type of diversity is seen as a threat to the status quo. Brett said, "My boss and I talked about how weird it was to go from L.A., where straight and gay couples socialize every day without even thinking about sexual orientation, to a place less than an hour away that could exist in certain parts of the Bible Belt. What we concluded was that no one in that particular city's leadership ever ventures far outside the area. In fact, most of them were born there and have never lived anywhere else. This combined with lower incomes results in a group-think mentality that produces a need to feel superior to anyone who can be classified as 'different.' And by different, I mean gay, black, brown, anyone that isn't white and an NRA member. I suppose I shouldn't generalize, but for the most part, I don't think I've ever met anyone in that area who went beyond high school, and that includes the mayor. The ironic thing is that a huge percentage of this particular city's residents are minority agricultural workers." He paused, then said, "I keep thinking how these city officials make fun of minorities, and then collect a paycheck that's furnished by the tax dollars of minority citizens. The hypocrisy is mind-blowing."

TALKING ABOUT . . . RETURNING TO AN UNFRIENDLY REGION

Six months after graduation, Jason, now twenty-nine and a successful hotel executive in Miami's South Beach, told me how returning to his parents' home to conduct a job search damaged his self-worth. "Toward the end, I was unbelievably depressed. I was starting to give up hope of ever finding a job—partly because I was ridiculed every day at home. If it wasn't my family saying that 'only queers live in

A homophobic living environment can sabotage your self-worth and your job search.

South Beach and work in hotels,' which is where I wanted to live and what I wanted to do, then it was the people I knew from high school. And, for the most part, none of them had moved forward. They were right where I left them when I went off to college."

Even though Jason was out of the closet at college, he wasn't out to anyone in his family. "I knew if I came home while I looked for a job that I'd have to go back into the closet. My friends tried to get me to stay in California, but I wanted to do whatever it took to work in South Beach. My family lives barely two hours from Miami, so at the time it seemed to make financial sense."

Four months after arriving home, Jason landed a job with a large hotel chain in the South Beach area and immediately moved to Miami. "My ties to my family are now pretty much nonexistent. My advice for anyone who's thinking about moving home to a family that is antigay is that it sets you up for all kinds of head trips that can hold you back. By the time I left, I felt unbelievably bad about myself."

Now, Jason told me, his partner's family has become his family too. He said, "I don't feel like an orphan anymore. I finally had to recognize that it's their issues and not mine that prevents them from loving me for me. Their old-time Baptist religion won't allow them to even think about how their beliefs are rooted in unfounded bigotry. I tried to have a conversation with my mother once about how bigotry, in any form, isn't about God, but about man. She wouldn't even consider the possibility that her religion is more about politics and power than spirituality and goodness." He paused before adding what I thought was a very insightful perspective on this issue, speaking from firsthand experience. "It's sad to think that someone uses God as a reason not to love their own child."

Overcoming the Effects of Religion-Based Homophobia

I recently had the opportunity to speak with an executive from a large aerospace company on the subject of religious-based homophobia in the workplace. He spoke with me on the condition that the name and location of the company wouldn't be revealed. As a key leader of the company's diversity initiative, it is interesting that he didn't feel free to speak openly without the assurance of anonymity (since this is what his job is all about). "The acceptance of gays and lesbians in our company differs like night and day between our white-collar and blue-collar workers, and between locations. The East and West Coasts are different worlds compared to the Midwest and the South." He told me that in his opinion, most of the people in the company's factory have no idea that the company even offers domestic partner benefits. "If they found out that anyone in their immediate environment was gay and using these benefits, I'm sure there'd be some kind of harassment or trouble. Whenever we have complaints of abuse based on sexual orientation, the offender almost always justifies his or her actions by claiming 'God doesn't like gays.' Part of my job is to ask the alleged offender why that is, and I've never been given a well-thought-out or logical answer. It's just, 'Because the Bible says so.' It's an irrational response, which makes it almost impossible to deal with. When I know someone gay is going into an area within our company that's known to be homophobic, I want to tell them to find the nearest exit and never look back. But I can't, because our policies state that we don't discriminate based on sexual orientation. In some places within the company that's true. In other places, it's a lie."

Intolerance for diversity often comes packaged with very conservative religious beliefs, and there's a clear connection between fundamentalist ideology and geographical homophobia. Dr. Elizabeth Davenport, the director of the Center for Women and Men at the University of Southern California, advocates for the rights of women in addition to those of the lesbian, gay, bisexual, and transgender community across the country. As an ordained minister in the Episcopal Church, she offers expert advice to the gay community when faced with religious-based bigotry in the workplace. "First, remember that not all religious people express negative attitudes toward lesbian and gay people. There are plenty of congregations out there who affirm and celebrate us for who we are, who bless our unions, who welcome us and our families. But ministers in more fundamentalist settings teach that any expression of sexuality other than plain vanilla heterosexual monogamy is morally wrong or—to use their word—sinful. If someone in your workplace believes this, the likelihood of you getting them to change their views anytime soon is not too great. They've been inculcated into ways of believing that define things as fixed systems, as good or bad. It takes a huge leap into critical thinking for them to understand the influence of Western dualism on their religious beliefs. The idea that sexual orientation might be morally neutral is quite foreign to them. In the end, I think that the hatred toward gay people that is endorsed by many conservative religious groups is not so much about sexual sin or guilt (I find fundamentalists happily ignorant of the odd things that the Bible says about proscribed heterosexual behaviors), but about control. It's about who's in and who's out, who's good and who's bad. And you can't control the beliefs of a religious person who upholds distorted ways of thinking about same-gender attraction any more than they can control your choices about how you live. Actually, that's the good news—you can control how you feel about yourself, how you act, how you believe."

As an authority on gender and sexual violence, she suggests that anyone who is experiencing workplace harassment because of their sexual orientation immediately become educated about the laws in their area. "Laws and workplace policies that provide protection to the LGBT community differ radically from location to location. I think it's important to know how far you will be protected or supported if you make a complaint. And if you're faced with religion-based harassment or discrimination in the workplace, document the specific behaviors that are discriminatory and then file a complaint in whatever way is open to you. I wouldn't necessarily advise engaging the offender in conversation about it right away. Because of the "good-bad" mind-set that underlies fundamentalist prejudices, it takes careful preparation and training to challenge it. Remember, Rosa Parks didn't just sit at the front of the bus one day because she couldn't find a seat at the back. She'd been involved in community-based training that prepared her to act and to face the consequences. So do the preparation. Find other LGBT folks in your workplace, or your city or town, and strategize together. And find straight allies in the organization who will support you and stand up for you. And never forget that God made you who you are, regardless of what you're being told by the offender. Celebrate it, rejoice in it, and live it! God made all of us in all our diversity."

TALKING ABOUT . . . RELIGIOUS PIETY

Glenn is a twenty-eight-year-old public administrator who recently moved from northern Florida, where he experienced a tremendous level of homophobic behavior in the workplace, back to his home in Southern California. When he graduated with a master's degree in public administration, the job that was most appealing to him turned out to be located in an area that was less than welcoming. "After my first week on the job, I knew I had made a mistake." Glenn told me that at times it seemed like most of the people he worked with were living on a different planet. "I had never lived in a city where almost everyone's life is dominated by the same religious views. When I went for the interview, I just figured that there was more to the area than fundamentalist picnics and rallies. But when I moved there and started my new job, I found out that half of the men belonged to this national group that was supposedly formed to make them better husbands and fathers. It's really an organization about bigotry and homophobia—and control." Several women in Glenn's office wanted to set him up on dates with their sisters, cousins, friends, and neighbors. He told me, "Because I didn't accept their offers, it immediately undermined my credibility with them as a manager and put the issue of my sexual orientation on the front burner." Glenn wasn't out at work and decided it was in his best interest to stay in the closet. "Their whole lives are based on such heterosexual images. Everything revolves around getting married to someone of the opposite sex and having children. I started to resent it. At that point, I knew I had to get out." He said that he felt the situation could have taken a definite turn for the worse if he had stayed. "Toward the end, the questions about my personal life started to take on an almost threatening tone, and 'church' and 'God' were inserted into every conversation. The one smart thing I finally did to stave off problems was to let everyone know I was planning to leave once I made the decision. After that, they didn't seem as interested in my sexual orientation, because I wasn't going to be around long enough to 'contaminate' their small-minded world. Without a doubt, it was the most sanctimonious group of bigots I've ever encountered. I was naive to think it didn't matter where I went to work as a gay man. It matters."

Overall, 29 percent of the people who responded to the study have experienced verbal or physical abuse in the workplace because of their sexual orientation. Recognizing the potential for abuse at work and adopting strategies to prevent and break away from these negative situations are invaluable to your mental, physical, and career health. Gay professionals who live in rural and conservative areas have experienced greater job dissatisfaction, increased instances of workplace abuse, and fewer opportunities for advancement. There's also a much higher percentage of people that are closeted in these areas, which ultimately prevents the type of freedom you need to achieve your highest possible level of success.

Enhancing Your Opportunities through Regional Demographics

On April 26, 2000, through the bold leadership of the state's governor at the time, Howard Dean, Vermont became the first state where gay couples could be joined together in civil unions, in a giant leap forward for gay couples seeking equality. In an interview with *The Advocate*, Governor Dean stated, "This . . . is about principle, and that principle is respect for everyone—and that is regardless of gender, ethnicity, sexual orientation, race, or any one of a number of factors that makes us different." Immediately Governor Dean, who was up for reelection at the time, was faced with a backlash campaign. The "Take Back Vermont" movement proved ineffective in defeating Dean, who was reelected six months later.

In exit polls conducted by Voter News Service, Governor Dean was supported as a candidate by two-thirds of the people with college degrees as well as in households where the income level was between $75,000 and $100,000. In addition, residents under the age of thirty, regardless of gender, did not view the civil union bill as a divisive issue. Also, in general, of people over age thirty, women were less opposed to gay marriage than men. Voters who identified themselves as fundamentalist Christians were, not surprisingly, the ones leading the unsuccessful "Take Back Vermont" campaign.

So, are all people who didn't go to college or reside in rural areas intolerant, uneducated extremists? Absolutely not. However, the opportunity to be exposed to and thereby educated about people with different ethnic backgrounds, cultures, religions, or sexual orientations is certainly limited when people choose to or are compelled to stay in one place. Be wary of locations that fit this profile. The bottom line is that your career will not be enhanced when you live and work in a region that believes you are "wrong" as a human being.

EXERCISE **Assessing Levels of Homophobia**

If you're considering accepting a job in an unfamiliar geographic location, these five steps can help you determine the potential for being out of the closet and successful at work and at home.

1. Go to the employment websites for the state, county, and city where you're considering working. The best-case scenario is that each government entity includes sexual orientation in their employment statements and provides domestic partner benefits. If none of these three entities provides welcoming workplace environments for the gay community, the likelihood that companies in the same location will be supportive is greatly reduced.

2. Review the Human Rights Campaign website at www.hrc.org to find out if the state, county, and city have hate crime laws. If there isn't any type of legal protection for victims of hate crimes based on sexual orientation, the reality may be that it isn't welcoming for gay people.

3. Network with members of the gay community who already reside in the area to determine the level of community acceptance. The Internet, including sites such as PlanetOut at www.planetout.com, provides the best access to networks for this purpose.

4. Visit the location. Go to the largest shopping mall in the area and become a watchful observer. Drive through the parking lot and look at bumper and window stickers. Do you see any symbols that suggest support of the gay community or are you overwhelmed with far-right slogans? If you're considering a specific employer, repeat this process in the employer's parking lot. Do you see gay couples out and about in restaurants, markets, and stores? Ask yourself if you'd be comfortable on a date or with a partner at a busy restaurant in the area. Be honest. If your answer is no, reevaluate why you would choose to live in a location where you're not welcome because of your sexual orientation.

5. Find out the educational demographics of the region's population. The U.S. Census Bureau website at www.census.gov lists the education level of the population for all states and counties. Examine the demographics of the regions you're considering as locations to live and work.

Relocating Is Not a Cop-Out

When you're employed in a region or city that isn't gay-friendly, the first order of business is to make the decision to explore career options in other locations. There's no other option if your goal is to achieve the highest possible level of professional success. Once you recognize that you have the power to change your circumstances, you can begin to break the cycle of environmental entrapment.

How many times have you heard someone say, "Running away never solved anything"? Leaving an employment situation or location because you're not allowed to be honest about who you are or because you feel that you may be in any type of danger is not running away. It's simply a wise personal and professional decision. But you have to do your research in order to make sure that your move will not set you up for a repeat performance of what you've just experienced. The exercises above and below will help you make an informed decision.

Overcoming Family Pressure to Return Home after College

As we've already learned from Jason's experience of returning home to look for a job after college, "Home Sweet Home" may not be everyone's reality. But family pressure to return home coupled with the typical economic needs of a recent college graduate may make the challenge of living somewhere else seem insurmountable. One way to avoid having to return to a negative environment is to have a job lined up that will allow you to be self-supporting. If you're in college or preparing to graduate, the following steps can help you avoid the need to return to an unfriendly environment where your ability to succeed may be limited.

- Visit your college career center with the goal of connecting to employers in locations you've identified as gay-friendly. If you have no idea what you want to do, chapter 10 will help guide you in how to make successful career decisions that will give you an equal or better chance to succeed as yourself.

- If you attend a college that welcomes gay diversity, connect with gay faculty and administrators as well as alumni to help you meet inclusive employers. Let them know you're looking for employment.

- If your college has a gay alumni association, connect with the leadership and ask them to help you identify mentors as well as gay alumni who may also be potential employers.

- When pressured by your family to return home, let them know you already have an effective career-planning strategy in place. Mention employers and jobs that you've researched as well as the salary you expect to earn. No matter how much they may want you to return home, it's difficult to discount the maturity and responsibility you'll demonstrate when taking ownership of your career and job search.

EXERCISE   **Will Relocating Benefit Your Career?**

Are you sacrificing success because of where you live? The following quiz can help you determine whether you should consider relocating to an area that's gay-friendly.

1. Do you feel local newspapers in your area would refuse to run a positive story about a company because it's gay owned?

2. If you were looking for a job in your area with organizations that offer domestic partner benefits, would your options be limited?

3. Do you feel the management of any restaurant near your home or workplace would refuse to host an event for a well-known gay rights organization?

4. Do you feel it might be necessary for members of the gay community near your home or workplace to present a "straight" persona when out in public to avoid harassment or violence?

5. Would placing a small rainbow sticker on one's car in your neighborhood present potential danger or harassment for the driver?

If you answered yes to any of these questions, I want you to imagine what it would be like to live in an area where you would be able to answer no without hesitation. The power you gain when you're no longer constrained by these types of limitations will provide you with the security and freedom to go out into the professional world and build a successful career as yourself.

Placing Yourself in a Positive and Affirming Environment

The decision to adapt to regional norms by pretending to be straight is a personal issue with varying meanings and consequences. For some members of the gay community, changing their identity to fit the standards of a region is not a choice under any circumstances. For others, the decision to avoid the issue of their sexual orientation at work is an issue of economics or a by-product of societal conditioning. But the bottom line is that a "don't ask, don't tell" policy doesn't affirm who you are. Built into this statement is the acknowledgment that you cannot tell the truth about who you are. Finding a better job, or first job, where you can be truthful with yourself and your employer is much easier and more productive than trying to survive in a bad professional situation where you're limited because you are gay. If you're in a workplace environment where you're not allowed to succeed, forced to hide, or, even worse, harassed verbally or physically, get out. Begin to look for a new job where your sexual orientation will provide additional value, not less. How do you start? The next chapter is all about making successful career decisions throughout your professional lifetime. You *can* achieve your highest possible level of success.

Finding Your
Perfect Employer

A GOOD FRIEND OF MINE WHO prides himself on owning all the latest trendy gadgets on the market recently bought a new car equipped with a satellite tracking system. When I flew to San Francisco for a business trip (just a few weeks after he drove the car off the showroom floor), he picked me up at the airport. Standing on the curb outside the terminal, I could tell how proud he was when he honked and waved to me from about a hundred yards away. Before I even had a chance to close my door and say hello, he pointed to the car's dashboard. Then, with the push of a button, our "guide" appeared, telling us where we were in the world. As you'd expect, we were in San Francisco.

My friend was eager to demonstrate the guide's powers, so he asked me to enter the address of our destination—a favorite restaurant in Chinatown. Even though he knew exactly where the restaurant was located, he insisted we use the navigation system. I entered the address, which he had already written down, and within a few seconds a golden map appeared that framed our perfect route. The map was designed for our particular road that afternoon, and it did in fact guide us to our destination quickly and without any angst. My friend was beaming as we pulled up to the restaurant. "It's all about being prepared. No matter where I am, it keeps me on track." Since I had just completed the first analysis of my research, I couldn't help but notice the similarity between my friend's navigation system and the development of a "navigation guide" that empowers the gay community to reach their desired professional destinations as quickly as possible and without any angst.

To develop your own "navigation guide," you'll need to focus on the question "How do I get there?" Where's there? It's where you'll be given an equal chance to succeed in the world of work and be valued because of who you are—a talented and skilled professional. It's where being gay is an asset because your sexual orientation is, in fact, part of what makes you unique. Together we're going to develop the criteria for creating a personalized guide for staying "on track" to achieve your highest possible level of lavender success. In its final form, your guide will empower you to identify career fields, organizations, and specific jobs that will provide you with the opportunity to succeed as yourself.

Building Your Seven Points of Success Framework

Your guide, representing your "perfect route" for making successful career decisions throughout your lifetime, will ultimately be based on the following seven points that will be joined together within a personalized framework (see page 105). As gay people in the world of work, not only do we need to address the same realities as everyone else who's competing for success in the job market, but we also have to address the role our sexual orientation plays in our quest. The Seven Points of Success incorporate everything that makes you unique. No one else will have the same guide to success, because no one else is you. As a constant and dynamic navigation tool, it will be relevant to all stages of your career. The framework is designed to be a practical tool that connects the two major determinants of a successful fit, your unique identity and your workplace environment. Your sexual orientation illuminates and influences each of the seven points, because, after all, it's part of who you are. Therefore, it's a significant factor in your career.

CONNECTING WHO YOU ARE WITH WHAT YOU DO

We'll start off by defining each of the Seven Points of Success, using the concepts that we've discussed in previous chapters. Remember that the goal is to accurately connect your unique identity with the right workplace environment so you can realize your professional dreams. Begin by spending a few minutes looking at the following diagram. It's not a complicated theory, and it's not about psychological counseling. It's simply about gathering together all the necessary information in one place in order to empower you to achieve your professional dreams.

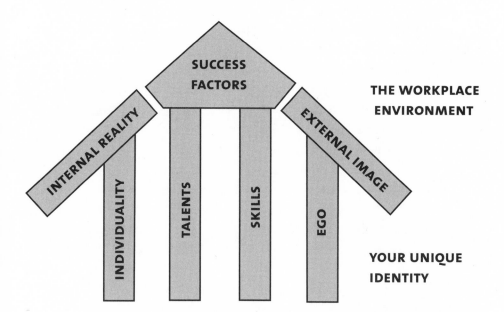

The first step is to become familiar with all of the major elements that make up your unique identity, described in points 1 to 4:

Point 1. Individuality: This point addresses who you are as a unique human being and includes your personal demographics. It includes your sexual orientation, gender, and ethnicity, as well as your innate personality and pertinent physical characteristics.

Point 2. Talents: This point addresses your natural abilities. For example, you may have been born with the ability to write and play music without ever having taken a lesson. You may have an instinctual flair for mathematics or science. Perhaps you're a natural-born storyteller. These are all examples of natural abilities or talents.

Point 3. Skills: This point addresses your learned abilities. These abilities are acquired through education and experience. The abilities to program a computer using a specific software product or make a medical diagnosis based on interpreting complicated tests, for example, are skills that you learn. Think of your skills as resume tangibles, those abilities you would list on a resume to describe your professional know-how.

Point 4. Ego: This point addresses the image you seek to portray to the world. It's about what's important to you, and how you want to live your life relative to your self-image. In this context, having an ego is not undesirable.

Now, let's move on to the workplace environment, which represents points 5 through 7. At this time, you may want to go back and quickly look at how your framework is structured, because each of the points in your unique identity has a correlating point within the workplace environment.

Point 5. Internal Reality: This point addresses how the workplace welcomes someone with your individuality. You'll use this point to determine if you will be given the opportunity to succeed within a particular employment situation.

Point 6. Success Factors: This point addresses the job requirements you need in order to be successful in a particular role within a particular organization, based on your natural and learned abilities (talents and skills). In other words, it's knowing what you need to be able to do in order to succeed on the job.

Point 7. External Image: This point addresses the way in which an organization, and therefore your role within that organization, is perceived by the external world. It's about finding out whether or not the image portrayed by the organization aligns with the image you seek to portray to the world. You need to be proud of what you do to be fully invested in your career.

FINDING YOUR PERFECT MATCH

Begin by thinking about each of the four points that make up your unique identity as pillars that hold up the roofline of the framework. As you can see in the diagram, your individuality and ego points are on each side, supporting the exterior of the framework. Together, your talents and skills combine to support your achievement in the workplace.

Visualize how the three points that make up your workplace environment (the roofline) are actually held in place by you. Successfully connecting your unique identity with the workplace environment means that you will always be strong enough to sustain the weight of the job. In other words, of course you can do it, because you're you.

Defining Your Unique Identity

As we go through each of the seven points, we will be discovering exactly what they mean relative to you and your professional goals. The Seven Points of Success will give you the ability to author, achieve, and sustain your highest possible level of success.

POINT 1: INDIVIDUALITY

If you've ever spent time with a large family, you've probably noticed how some family members seem like they're from different planets. Just like those sisters and brothers who seem so different from one another, you are also like no one else. This first point addresses the importance of recognizing your personal demographics in order to find a successful career fit.

EXERCISE **It All Starts with You**

> *Write down your answers to each of the following questions. You'll refer back to your answers later in the book, when we use them to transform your career goals into career achievements.*

> 1. Identify your sexual orientation, gender, and ethnicity. Your basic demographic realities have extreme relevance in the world of work. For example, if people who share some or all of your attributes are already successful within an organization, then it's likely that you, too, will be given a chance to thrive.

> 2. Describe your innate personality, selecting three to five adjectives that best characterize your "natural self." For example, you may be naturally optimistic, pessimistic, gregarious, a loner, energetic, or methodical in your approach to life. Aligning your natural character with the personality of the workplace environment will allow you to work in harmony with the organization to achieve your goals, and theirs.

> 3. Assess the status of your health and sensory abilities. Many people have certain physical limitations that need to be considered in their professional life. For example, if you have vision, hearing, or movement impairment, these conditions should be considered when determining whether or not you'll be given an equal chance to succeed. Challenges such as attention deficit disorder and dyslexia should also be considered and recognized.

POINTS 2 AND 3: TALENTS AND SKILLS

Talents are natural gifts. A beautiful singing voice, athletic prowess, an instinctual understanding of the human condition, and the ability to effectively communicate with others are just a few of the endless talents people are born with and use to their professional advantage. Skills are learned abilities you acquire through education or professional experience. The ability to conduct an IRS-approved financial audit is an example of a skill. As depicted in the Seven Points of Success, your talents and skills combine to satisfy the requirements of the job.

EXERCISE **Integrating Your Abilities to Maximize Your Success**

1. Think about those activities in which you've always excelled and put together a list of your talents. Remember that everyone is born with natural gifts, and you may be taking yours for granted. Think about hobbies or work-related activities that make you lose all track of time. When we choose to do something in our spare time, there's a good chance that we're good at it.

2. List three or more activities you have excelled at in your lifetime, beginning in childhood. For example, you may have been a competitive runner in high school or college, or you may currently be a great cook or baker. Friends and family may have told you that you are a "natural-born peacekeeper." Your list will help you to identify an important part of your overall portfolio of abilities.

3. If you were to teach a course for either college students or professional adults, for academic or personal enrichment, what would the subject be and what would your teacher evaluations say about you? Your responses can help you identify those areas where you feel you're an authority and further develop your resume tangibles.

POINT 4: EGO

Does it matter what others think about you? In the workplace, the answer is a resounding "yes." Every day people are hired, promoted, and fired because of how others view them as individuals and professionals. For the gay community, placing yourself in an environment where your sexual orientation is not an issue is necessary for achieving success, but it will not prevent you from being evaluated by others. The image you portray to the world, like everyone else, gay or straight, makes a difference in the workplace. The image you would like to portray is defined within the context of the framework as your ego. Most of us have been told at one time or another that having an ego is undesirable, but the only real negative associated with the term *ego* is not giving it the value it deserves when it comes to making career decisions.

As you define your unique identity, you're also defining how you want the world to see you. Begin by eliminating any preconceived ideas that your ego, as it affects your career decisions, is either good or bad. For example, if it's important for you to be viewed as someone who recognizes and enjoys the finer things in life, don't shy away from that fact because you think others will judge you. In fact, if prestige is important to you, working for a renowned firm with a well-respected name will give you a strong match between your ego point and the external image of the workplace environment. If you want to be known as someone whose life work is dedicated to making the world a better place, then being part of a multinational conglomerate known for raiding smaller companies and putting people out of work will put this part of your unique identity at odds with the workplace environment. When you identify your ego point, you're giving yourself real-life facts that empower you to determine if a job will give you what you need in order to be proud of what you do.

EXERCISE **Your Image Matters**

1. Write down the names of the three people you most admire professionally. What do you believe is their professional mission? Your answers will provide you with insight into what you value in other people in the world of work, as well as what type of self-image is important to you.

2. Identify a few words or short phrases that colleagues and peers would use to describe you as a professional. Your answers will determine if your career path until now supports the image you wish to be known for. Ask yourself if there are similarities between how others describe you and how you describe those professionals you most admire.

Defining the Workplace Environment

You're getting close to completing the Seven Points of Success, so keep moving toward the finish line! Now that you've defined the four points that make up your unique identity, you have the necessary information to determine if a particular workplace environment will provide you with an opportunity to succeed. The three points that make up the workplace environment get to the heart of what an organization is really all about.

For the purpose of completing the next set of exercises, you can use your current employer or substitute a potential employer. If you use your current employer, you can determine where you are successfully matched in your job or conversely, find out where you may be "disconnected." If you use a potential employer, perhaps one that you're carefully considering or just exploring as a possibility, you can use the exercises to predict whether or not the employer is a good match. The important thing is to consider all of the seven points in order to understand how they work together as the basis for creating your personalized guide.

POINT 5: INTERNAL REALITY

Many companies sound great in their recruiting materials and websites, with a workforce that appears diverse and happy. Keep in mind that all of these glossy materials with smiling employees are part of each company's public relations machine. The reality of what goes on inside the organization may be very different from what those images depict.

EXERCISE **Are There Other Gay People Here?**

To find out if the internal reality of an organization is a good match for your individuality, take a demographic inventory of the organization's leadership. This approach will give you real-life information about who's being hired and promoted within the organization and will help you determine if you will be valued there.

1. Are high-level positions within the organization held by people who have diverse personal demographics? If your answer is "yes," name each person along with their respective job titles. Then, briefly describe what you know about their individualities. If your answer is "no," identify whether or not there are employees at *any* level with diverse personal demographics.

2. Does the organization support philanthropic causes that are inclusive of the gay community? If it's a larger company, check out the Human Rights Campaign's equality index on their website at www.hrc.org.

For smaller companies, use the same criteria listed on HRC's site to determine their equality index score. Write down how the organization does or does not support the gay community.

3. What words or phrases would you use to describe the energy level or corporate atmosphere within the organization? For example, are the employees pleasant and energetic? Are they cold and unhappy? If possible, find a good vantage point and observe people leaving the organization at the end of the workday. Do you notice camaraderie and smiles as they say good-bye? Or do they rush to their cars one by one, barely acknowledging each other before tearing out of the parking lot?

4. Based on what you've observed and discovered about the organization, do you believe an employee would feel comfortable placing a photo of a same-sex partner on their desk? List the reasons why you would or would not feel comfortable.

POINT 6: SUCCESS FACTORS

The Seven Points of Success framework is all about setting yourself up to achieve. Defining the success factors of a job is all about understanding how points two and three, your talents and skills, provide you with the ability to succeed in that particular job. To a great extent, when people who possess talents and skills similar to your own are successful within an organization, you'll likely have the abilities needed to succeed.

EXERCISE **Knowing What It Takes to Get Recognized**

When you are able to measure your potential for success based on the requirements of a job, you can substantially increase your chances of finding the right professional match. Your goal is to find out what an employer is really looking for in successful employees. Discovering the success factors of a job empowers you to succeed.

1. Identify who's successful within the organization. List three leaders and describe their talents and skills, as you perceive them. If this is a new or potential employer, identify them in terms of their job descriptions, titles, and where they fall within the organization's hierarchy.

2. Are the job functions of people who are successful within the organization tied to traditional gender roles? List several key organizational players along with their job titles. Then describe how their functions do or do not conform to traditional gender roles.

3. Identify three ways your talents and skills can help the organization accomplish its goals. Think about how the talents and skills of those who are successful within the workplace contribute to the organization's overall goals.

POINT 7: EXTERNAL IMAGE

Because the definition of success is completely subjective, each of us must define it for ourselves and decide what we need professionally in order to be fulfilled. However, there's a common thread that runs through each person's unique definition of success. Our personal image is connected to and affected by the image of our employer.

The image that a workplace projects not only impacts how you feel about yourself, but it also impacts the quality of your work.

Have you ever been less than proud about working for an organization but had no choice because you had to pay the rent? Many people I interviewed told me they feel that what's important to them in their life has nothing at all to do with what's important to their employer. For these people, it logically follows that they will not be giving their all to that particular job—not because they're lazy, but because the job provides them with no sense of fulfillment. As a result, there's a disconnect between who they are and what they do in their professional lives.

EXERCISE **Being Proud of What You Do**

Aligning yourself with the right workplace environment and feeling good about where you work requires you to determine if the external image of an organization will support and add value to your life based on your ego point. In order to become fully aware of the public perception of an organization, visit the PR Newswire at www.prnewswire.com and Hoover's Online at www.hooversonline.com to find bits of information that the organization has recently publicized. In addition, an online search engine will quickly lead you to reviews, editorials, and newspaper and magazine articles that will help you determine how an organization is portrayed. Take a look at the information that's out there and then complete the following questions. You'll use your answers to determine whether that external image is a match with your own ego.

1. Based on the material you reviewed about the organization, describe its public persona by using one- or two-word phrases like progressive, cutting-edge, uptight, or defensive.

2. Describe how you think the organization's top leader would define its mission in a television interview if forced to tell the truth. This will give you specific criteria to gauge how well the spin matches the reality.

3. Identify three actions that the organization is performing in order to accomplish its publicly stated mission. Your answers will help you assess the level at which your own ego can be enhanced and supported through the direction of the organization.

4. If you were asked to represent the gay community in a national public service announcement promoting workplace equality, what would you say about this organization? List the main points of your "commercial." Whether positive or negative, they should represent your truthful opinion of how welcoming this organization is for the gay community.

Achieving Success Because of Who You Are

Having all of the facts is only part of the solution to achieving your highest possible level of success. Success also requires that you get honest with yourself. All of the people that you've already met and will continue to meet in this book who have created their own brand of success have taken an honest look at themselves in the mirror and done the work to get to a place where they feel good about being gay. Like my friend Sally taught us, our difference is our strength.

When you're hired into a new job, the employer hires you because you are the best person for the job. If you're out of the closet and hired into an organization that values its gay employees, your sexual orientation is part of the whole person that was hired. It's a great feeling to go into a job knowing you have an equal chance to succeed. It's an even better feeling to know that since the "whole person" includes your individuality and, therefore, your sexual orientation, you can honestly say that you were hired *because* you're gay.

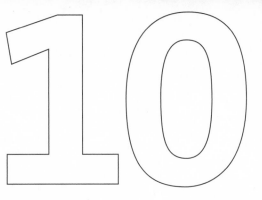

Out of the Closet and into a Successful Career

BEING OUT OF THE CLOSET IN YOUR PROFESSIONAL LIFE means that you have the freedom to create your success based on your true self. Being out shifts the balance of power in your favor and puts you—not the employer or society—in control of your career. Whether you're looking for your first job, moving up in your current field, or making a transition into an entirely new career, the positive dynamics you'll experience from being out of the closet during your job search will benefit your career today, tomorrow, and throughout your professional lifetime.

Your decision to be out of the closet at work affects your approach to getting a new job due to these four factors:

- Your emotional outlook surrounding the job search process shifts from fear and avoidance to empowerment and optimism.

- Your resume will reflect the real you, and it can include gay-related volunteer activities and organizations that can translate into valuable career skills.

- In an interview you can completely focus on how your talents and skills meet the requirements of the job, without the worry of hiding your sexual orientation.

- When you feel good about yourself, you place a higher value on your abilities, which translates into increased salary dollars.

Turning Fear and Avoidance into Empowerment and Optimism

The first career event I organized for gay students at USC brought gay alumni from a wide variety of fields and industries back to campus, and also attracted employers that welcome gay employees. At the end of the program, as the panel wrapped up their final comments, a student jumped out of her seat and ran up to me with tears in her eyes. I'll never forget what she said to me, because it was the catalyst for the research that led to this book. "I didn't think anyone would want me to work for them," she said. Her tears were a mixture of emotions—a release of past fears, a surprising new sense of self-worth, and hope for the future. "I'm a black gay female, and I didn't know anyone in the professional world cared about my dreams." Seeing a panel of successful and out lesbians and gay men, as well as straight allies, representing some of the top companies in the world gave her the evidence and knowledge she needed to transform her fears into hope. Several weeks later the same young woman dropped by my office full of excitement. She told me that she had written a letter to one of the panelists and was meeting with him about a summer internship. Why was she suddenly empowered to go out into the professional world and successfully present herself to an employer? Because she found out that she was valuable.

TALKING ABOUT . . . FEAR

"The only thing worse than working for a family-run business is working for a family-run business that isn't owned by your own family!" Nell is a successful twenty-seven-year-old copywriter for a gay-friendly advertising firm in Monterey, California. Today she's out of the closet in her professional life, but the negative experiences of her last job are, in her words, "finally becoming part of my emotional past, and not my daily experience."

Nell accepted a position as an advertising coordinator with a family-owned and -operated health-care business that employs nearly two hundred people. During her job search, the idea of connecting her individuality with the internal reality of a company where she could succeed as herself was the last thing on Nell's mind. "Even though I was out to my parents and close friends, I was afraid to be out at work, particularly when I was looking for a job." When I asked her why she was afraid, she said, "One reason is because my family still tells me to this day that I'm going to have a difficult life because I'm gay. And until recently, I believed them. In their own way, they mean well. But for a long time, it totally made me feel like no one would want to hire me if they knew I was gay." What Nell's family should have said to her was that it doesn't have to be difficult; it just depends on the choices you make and whether or not you believe in yourself.

Nell told me that all kinds of "warning bells and whistles" went off during the three interviews it took to land the job with the family-run healthcare company. However, she ignored all of them, including a phone call from someone inside the company who told her that the owners "encouraged" everyone to attend their fundamentalist church. "I wanted a job in advertising so much that I didn't listen to my own instincts. I was afraid not to go along with whatever the owners wanted or expected me to be, and it turned out to be terrible."

Being true to yourself gives you the chance to manage your own fate.

When you're looking for a job as someone you're not, you put the job itself in control. When that happens, the disconnect between who you are and what you do can cultivate feelings of fear, anxiety, and even anger. As soon as these feelings enter the workplace, and they will, it becomes impossible to truly succeed.

Nell stayed in the position for fourteen months, spending the last two in an intensive job search that ended with an offer from her current employer, where she's comfortably out of the closet. "After two months in the other job, I couldn't sleep. After four months, I couldn't eat. And after six months, I stopped laughing and having fun. To be honest, it felt like I was suffocating." With the help of a good therapist, Nell slowly began to feel like there was indeed hope for her professional future. "I guess my advice for someone who's working in a place that's oppressive is to put yourself first. When you do, the only choice that really makes sense is to look for another job—fast. If you're gay, surround yourself with people who are out at home, at the office, even at the supermarket! And make sure they like themselves. Seeing other people who are doing what they want to do, and being true to themselves, will give you hope."

Making Your Sexual Orientation a Workplace Asset

For the gay community, our life experiences result in professional gains just from walking along our own individual paths. These experiences can also be considered assets on the job market. For example, coming out to family and friends is arguably one of the most delicate acts of communication any human being can perform. If you ask employers what they're looking for, and I ask several hundred each year, nine times out of ten their answer is "communication skills." Although I'm not suggesting you recite your own coming out story during interviews, think about how your own path has enhanced your professional value. When you do, you'll discover how being gay provides you with special skills and abilities that will add to your value.

EXERCISE **_Determining Why Being Gay Is an Asset_**

It's time for you to understand more about your unique professional value as a member of the gay community. Right now, begin to think about how your sexual orientation can allow you to work better and be more competitive in the professional world. Create a value-added list that describes how your life experiences as a gay person can translate into real value for an employer. Begin by concentrating on the three skill sets listed below that employers look for in job candidates, and write down how being gay has required you to excel in these three areas. Your results from this exercise can change the way you view yourself professionally, which in turn will make a positive impact on how you present yourself to a potential employer. As you develop your value-added list, think in terms of how being gay has improved your skills in each area.

1. Communication Skills

2. Critical Thinking Skills

3. Creative Problem-Solving Skills

Approaching New Opportunities as Yourself

Let me ask you a question. Have you ever stopped yourself from listing an affiliation on your resume because it might be interpreted as gay? If you're pursuing employment with companies and organizations where your sexual orientation is a nonissue, then you will never need to edit any aspect of your unique identity. Remember that the purpose of a resume is to help you land an interview. And you don't want to interview with an employer who doesn't want gay people in the workplace. When clients ask me if they should hide the truth on their resume, my response is always the same: "How successful can you be if the person they hire doesn't exist?" Not having the freedom to be yourself will always keep you on the defensive, and that's not the best mind-set to have when you're putting your resume together, interviewing, and negotiating an offer.

TALKING ABOUT . . . BEING YOURSELF

Andy is a twenty-four-year-old human resources consultant who has always been out of the closet in both his personal and professional life. I knew Andy as a student and he always incorporated his unique identity into his class projects. When I interviewed him for this book, I found out something I hadn't known before. He told me, "In my senior year of college, a professor in the business school told me that I should make my resume 'less gay.' I know she was trying to help, but suggesting I take off my volunteer work at the university as an HIV educator was, first of all, ignorant, because HIV isn't a gay disease. Second, taking it off it would mean that the skills I acquired as a result of my experience wouldn't bring any value to an employer."

Having been in my class, Andy knew that this simply wasn't true. In fact, in his current job, Andy uses the skills he acquired in his volunteer position every day, counseling people about their benefit plans and retirement packages. Andy said, "I didn't take her advice. I left my volunteer work on my resume and I know that's one of the reasons I was hired. It was totally relevant to my current job. If someone wants to think less of me as a job candidate because I've accomplished something that might be considered 'gay,' then my choice would be to move on. My resume is about me, and if someone wants to infer that I'm gay because of something I've done professionally, that's fine. I am gay!"

Writing a Brilliant Resume

There are several excellent resume books on the market, and one I use both at the university and in my private practice is *Damn Good Resume Guide*, by Yana Parker (Ten Speed Press, 2002). Most of the major job search websites, including monster.com, monstertrak.com, and careerbuilder.com, also have quality examples of resumes. The main thing you want to remember is to be consistent. Whether you center your name and address or justify it to one side, and whether you list dates in the left margin or place them directly after the name of an employer, are completely subjective decisions and should always reflect your own good taste. There is no right or wrong way to do it, but you do need to be consistent in your presentation.

Once you have reviewed sample resumes from the sources I've mentioned, choose a format that you like. Next, use the Seven Points of Success exercises from chapter 9 to give you ideas about what talents and skills you want to highlight to a potential employer. Don't forget to incorporate aspects of your description of how being gay is an asset relative to the three things employers look for most in job candidates: communication skills, critical thinking skills, and creative problem-solving skills.

Here are a few final guidelines for creating an effective resume:

- Have someone in the field review your resume before you send it out. Your networking contacts who are professionals in your field of interest can fill you in on what types of talents and skills are most appealing to hiring managers within their industry.

- Avoid using any creative email address on a resume. I've personally received resumes with email names such as "pimpdaddy," "sugarthighs," and "butternuts." None of them got a call for an interview. The email address on your resume should reflect your legal name or a combination of your initials and name, period.

- Choose a font that's familiar to most readers, and make sure it's large enough to read and scan easily. Stay away from anything smaller than an eleven-point font.

- Perform a double, triple, and quadruple check for spelling and grammar errors. Employers report that these common errors are used to eliminate you as a viable candidate more than any other reason.

- Keep copies of every cover letter and resume you send out. When you get called in for an interview, you'll want to refer back to the exact information you sent to an employer.

- Finally, make sure that there is no blaring music or celebrity impersonation on your outgoing voice mail recording. If someone calls you to arrange an interview and they get a rock star, they'll probably hang up without leaving a message. You'd be surprised how many job interviews never take place because this initial opportunity to make a good impression is lost.

Communicating Your Value in an Interview

Interviews are about communicating your value to an employer and convincing her that you're the best person for the job. If you spend time scripting all kinds of false responses to possible questions in order to hide your sexual orientation, then you are editing your unique identity. You'll never be able to thoroughly communicate how your talents and skills are a perfect match for the requirements of the job if you're portraying someone who doesn't exist. And if they don't want gay people in their workplace, you don't want to be there either.

Fourteen percent of survey respondents left their last position because the workplace environment wasn't gay-friendly. Some people noted poor working relationships with other employees or supervisors, while others cited an overall lack of opportunities for gay people. The majority of people in this category attempted to hide their sexual orientation, beginning with the interview.

The most likely scenario leading up to your interview with a potential employer is that your resume and networking contacts got you in the door. Now you want to successfully communicate your qualifications and ability to fit in with the existing workforce. Nonverbal communication plays a substantial role in how you're perceived by employers once you're in their office. Your clothing, body language, eye contact, and posture can all convey a sense of confidence and friendliness once you have face time with an employer. In addition to evaluating your ability to meet the requirements of the job, potential employers use many nonverbal cues to help decide whether you're someone they want to spend their day with. You absolutely want to make a positive impression, but you also want to be yourself. In other words, it's like a first date. You simply want them to see you at your best!

Once you've been invited to meet with a potential employer, keeping in mind these dos and don'ts will help you successfully navigate the interview:

- Do prepare yourself by learning about the organization. Familiarize yourself with their mission statement and any new business developments they are involved in, such as recent acquisitions or product launches.

- Don't try to know more than the person interviewing you. No one likes a know-it-all, regardless of whether they're gay or straight.

- Do make a list of intelligent questions that you can ask the interviewer. This is the perfect time to learn about the diversity of the organization and whether gay employees are provided equal opportunities. Ask specific questions about the organization's mission and values.

- Don't ask about salary in the first interview unless the employer brings it up. If you're pressed for an answer, give a salary range that you know is appropriate for the opportunity. In addition to using your network to discover realistic salary expectations, you can also refer to the following websites for information about what compensation you might expect for specific jobs in specific locations: www.salary.com and www.salaryexpert.com.

- Do follow up after an interview with a thank-you note or email. If you have a panel interview, don't write the exact same message for each member of the panel. The recipients will compare, and you'll lose points for creativity if each one is identical.

Negotiating a Higher Salary

When it comes to negotiating salary, being yourself and believing in your value can translate into more money. As we've already discussed, many people feel that they deserve less because of their sexual orientation. That's a false idea put out into the world by people who don't want you to succeed. But, beyond the issue of sexual orientation, self-doubt can sneak up on anyone when it comes to negotiating salary. In other words, almost everyone gets anxious when it comes to asking for more money, whether it's a new job or a raise discussion. When you get a case of "salary doubt," remember that you're being made an offer because you're the best person for the job, and the best often costs a little bit more than the rest. Employers know that throughout the salary negotiation your goal is to continue putting your best foot forward, which usually works to their advantage. Therefore, in order to make sure that you get the best offer possible, including all of the benefits, vacation time, and possibly even a signing bonus that goes along with the position, be confident in your value and negotiate from facts. Remember, they want *you*.

TALKING ABOUT . . . GETTING A RAISE

Over the past ten years Kara has enjoyed three upward career moves within the same company. She's out of the closet in a positive workplace environment, and she is one of the leaders of the company's gay employee resource group. Although she has the opportunity to be successful based on her talents and skills, and isn't held back at all because of her sexual orientation, she hasn't been able to negotiate a salary that's appropriate for her position. "Maybe it's just that old habits die hard, but whenever I get the call telling me I got a new job, I'm already saying 'yes' before I've even heard how much money is involved. If I ran my career like I run my division, I probably wouldn't have accepted my last promotion, because my salary doesn't really reflect the extra work and responsibility that came with my new position. I've talked to my boss about it, and he knows that if I don't receive a substantial increase that puts me at the same level with my peers at other companies, then I'm going to move on. I know I'm valuable, but it's time to reflect that value in my paycheck!"

Historically, many members of minority communities have settled for less in their professional lives because they're simply grateful to be accepted by their employers. When I asked Kara if the rush of being accepted was one of the reasons she always takes the first offer, she said, "That's what I mean by 'old habits die hard.' For a lot of people who grew up gay, you have to fight against the feeling of being less-than. And 'less-thans' don't get paid as much as everyone else. Even though I'm successful, asking for more money is something I struggle with all the time."

Three months after our interview, Kara sent me an email telling me she had gotten her increase in salary. "Of course, I deserve more," she wrote, "but I can honestly say I'm now being paid the market rate for someone at my level, and it feels great!" When you're out of the closet professionally and feel good about who you are in the world, you are empowered to negotiate a fair and equitable salary. Remember that the employer made you the offer, probably choosing you over countless other candidates. There's no need to believe that the offer will disappear if you approach the negotiation process with factual salary data and enthusiasm for your new job.

Becoming Your Own Gay-Friendly Employer through Entrepreneurship

Owning your own business is a way to create your workplace environment. I asked all of the respondents who were entrepreneurs the same question: "To what extent was your sexual orientation a factor in making the decision to start your own business?" The overwhelming majority of people told me that their sexual orientation played a major role in motivating them to take the self-employment plunge.

TALKING ABOUT . . . BEING YOUR OWN BOSS

Sam, a successful thirty-three-year-old real estate developer, started his own company after spending five years with a large land company in Orange County, California. "When I started my career in a corporate setting, I didn't think of myself as being limited because I was gay since, at the time, I wasn't out. But looking back on my time with the company, there wasn't much of a connection between me and the people I worked with." Sam told me that as he grew more comfortable with himself and his sexual orientation, he grew less comfortable at work, and the idea of becoming his own boss became incredibly appealing. Today, after being out of the closet for several years in his own successful real estate business, he has gained what he describes as "hindsight smarts." He told me, "Without acknowledging it to anyone else, maybe even to myself, the main reason I left to start my own business was to have the freedom to be myself in a field that's very homophobic. Looking back, I'd say that if I were straight, I never would have left the company. But the way the company was at that time, and still is as far as I can tell, I could never be happy there. In my own company, the issue of being gay or straight just doesn't exist."

Like many gay entrepreneurs, Sam decided to be his own boss in part because of an instinctual drive to remove the issue of sexual orientation from his workplace environment. Whether limitations in your field because of your sexual orientation are perceived or real, acknowledged or ignored, if you feel like you can't come out of the closet, your instincts are probably right. Owning your own business has been one avenue that gay people have taken in order to overcome professional discrimination based on sexual orientation. However, becoming an entrepreneur isn't the cure-all for conquering homophobia, and independent gay business owners need to be aware of the potential

You can live your professional dreams when you're equipped with the right knowledge and resources, whether you're part of an existing organization or heading up your own company.

for homophobia when it comes to defining their client base. If you want to become an entrepreneur, do your homework and carefully prepare and evaluate your business plan. Above all, you need to believe in yourself 100 percent and be committed to the business 24/7.

• • •

The knowledge that you can succeed based on who you are as a whole human being will continually reinforce your own professional belief that gay is okay. In the same way that negative societal influences and homophobic workplace environments reinforce each other and limit your success, a gay-friendly workplace combined with your understanding of how you're more competitive because of your sexual orientation creates a synergy that results in your potential for unlimited success.

For members of the gay community who choose to no longer be closeted at work, a newfound sense of freedom and self-worth provides increased clarity about how they're choosing to spend their time on the job and at home. Finding career opportunities where you can be free of workplace discrimination is not only a possibility but a reality. When you have confidence in yourself and own the belief that you deserve success, you will be empowered to identify, interview for, and land your perfect job. It's vital to your professional health to always listen to your instincts about what's right for you, and then follow that intuitive road to success.

Enjoying Your Road to Success

ENJOYING YOUR ROAD TO SUCCESS is as important as arriving at your destination. Each networking contact you make, each fact about yourself you discover, and each opportunity you explore is an achievement. It's critical to recognize that success is not just a blurred vision that only exists in the future. You can start enjoying success today if you're able to recognize the value of your journey along the path itself.

While writing this book, I was a presenter at Workplace Summit, an annual event sponsored by Out & Equal Workplace Advocates, a nonprofit organization that provides services and programs designed to promote equality for all individuals, especially the LGBT community, families, and allies, in the workplace. Over a period of three days there *Wherever you may be on your career path, your success can begin right now.* were more than sixty workshops presented by human resources professionals and LGBT workplace leaders from around the country. Like all presenters, I was ranked by my audience on content as well as effectiveness of delivery. Since it was the first time I had presented the qualitative part of my research, I was anxious to read the evaluations. The following day, I picked up my ratings and found a quiet spot to look them over.

As I read the positive responses, I realized that each one was a successful achievement for me in the present. My longer-term goal of interpreting and bringing together all of my research in one book could easily become one of those blurred visions. Therefore, it was critical to the achievement of my longer-term goal to recognize each positive evaluation as a success. If you postpone acknowledging your success until you achieve your longer-term goal, it's quite possible you won't find the joy you expected when you get there, because the road itself hasn't provided you with any ongoing satisfaction. In other words, give yourself credit for each achievement, each day. They play an important role in your career.

Acknowledging Present Success

At the same Out & Equal conference, Howard Dean, then governor of Vermont, whom I noted in chapter 8 for signing this country's first civil union bill, delivered a keynote address that gave everyone in the audience fuel for continuing toward our shared long-term goal of workplace equality. In his address, Governor Dean pointed out how the recognition of same-sex marriage in Vermont was a success that would have been unimaginable even a few years ago. It was his acknowledgment of this

Each success along your journey contributes to the achievement of your long-term career goals.

accomplishment that helped everyone in the audience realize that it's okay to stop and give yourself credit for a job well done as we continue toward our long-term goals. When you give yourself credit for being on the road to success, you gain the expectation and belief that you can achieve your dreams. When everyone left the auditorium to go into various workshops and exhibits, we were more committed than ever to the journey because we *expected and believed* that workplace equality can be achieved.

TALKING ABOUT . . . PRESENT SUCCESS

"Medical students have no life!" That's the first sentence Victor wrote in an email to me after he volunteered for a one-on-one interview. "For me, it isn't about the present," he said. "Until you're a doctor, you're just a scrub!" At twenty-five, Victor is on his way to fulfilling his lifelong dream of becoming a physician. Out of the closet to everyone at work and at home, he plans to dedicate his practice to the elderly gay community. When we met in person for our interview, I asked him why he had selected this particular professional focus. He told me, "A lot of older gay people have been dismissed by their families and society and are hesitant to seek out medical help because they think no one cares. I know, because it happened in my own family."

If you ask incoming medical students why they want to become doctors, you'll often find some very personal reasons that led them into the field. In Victor's case, it was his grandfather's experience as an early victim of AIDS that motivated him to pursue medicine. "To be blunt, my grandfather was left for dead by most of my family, and he felt there wasn't anyone or anywhere to turn for help. As I got older and began to understand firsthand what it means to be gay in a straight world, I decided to do something about it."

Victor's drive and ambition propelled him forward in the pursuit of his goal of becoming a doctor. After he graduated with honors from USC, he was accepted into one of the country's leading medical schools. He told me that since the age of fifteen, he has worked to help fund his own professional dream, but he has neglected to give himself credit for all of his successes along the way.

"I'm always focused on the future, never the present, other than to complete whatever task is at hand that moves me closer to my dream. When I'm particularly stressed out, I'll lie awake at night and wonder if it will all be worth it when I get there." He took a minute to think about what he had revealed, and then he said, "It isn't much fun to always be living for the future. Sometimes it feels like the future will never come."

EXERCISE **Becoming an Achiever**

> To determine whether you're spending too much time thinking about the future and not enough time being successful in the present, create a balance sheet that measures your "career path productivity." Begin by giving yourself a total of 100 percent. Then, assign approximate percentages to the amount of time and energy you spend on the following six areas per week.

1. Worrying about your professional future

2. Managing your future

3. Measuring your success against the success of others

4. Developing or pursuing new ideas and strategies for achieving short-term career goals

5. Solving existing problems that impede your professional growth

6. Growing or building your talents and skills

Now create a pie chart based on these percentages. If you spend more than 25 percent of your time on tasks 1 through 3, there's an imbalance in the time you spend on the present versus the future. You can reverse this pattern by consciously spending more time on tasks 4 through 6. The time you spend on your career in the present yields real-time success. You'll be amazed that the more time you spend on tasks 4 through 6, the better you'll feel about yourself. And by achieving today you'll be giving yourself the encouragement you need to achieve your long-term goals in the future.

Accepting Support

No one reaches a professional goal without help. We've all seen a skit or comedy routine on television depicting a narcissistic actor telling the world on Oscar night that he or she did it all on his or her own! In the world of work, just like in Hollywood, nothing could be further from the truth.

As well as being aware that individual success is the result of group effort, you should also recognize that your dream may not be everyone else's dream. Labeling one dream as better than another is counterproductive to moving forward individually and as a community. Dreams are, and should be, completely subjective. For example, if your professional dream involves achieving financial wealth, it's important to remember that it's just as valuable to dream of working for a nonprofit organization dedicated to AIDS services or to be part of a struggling ballet company looking for their first big hit. All professional dreams are equal, and it's our obligation to others in the community to support those dreams in all of their diversity. In doing so, you'll open more doors for yourself, and help to eliminate discrimination in all workplaces.

TALKING ABOUT . . . DOING IT ALL YOURSELF

Feeling like you have to do it all yourself is a tremendous burden. Kent, a thirty-four-year-old pharmacist in Long Beach, California, completed his education believing that it was his "duty" to make his professional dreams come true all by himself. Kent, the second son of Korean immigrants, told me that his parents worked extremely hard to send their children to college.

"In our family, success meant not asking anyone for help, and that was the model I lived by for most of my life." Throughout his childhood, both of Kent's parents worked full-time at the same time they attended college. And in keeping with the tradition of their culture, his mother also managed the family at home. "I don't think my parents ever slept, but they also never complained. My oldest brother graduated from high school at the same time my father graduated from college, and, still, I never heard anyone say they were proud of what had been achieved. It was just expected."

Although he maintained an A average in high school, he was never praised for this achievement because, again, it was simply expected of him. He told me, "Grades were simply viewed as a tool to get into the right college." When he entered USC, his pattern of feeling entirely responsible for every aspect of his life continued. "I didn't feel like I should ask a professor for too much help, because I should be capable of figuring things out for myself. In my mind, asking for help was a sign of weakness."

Kent told me that in his senior year of college he began to explore his sexual identity, which until that time he had completely suppressed. "Going to a gay bar was too frightening, so instead I opted for a gay coffeehouse in West Hollywood. At first I was too afraid to talk to anyone, but slowly I started to meet people and developed a new set of friends beyond school. Until then, I didn't believe that other kids' parents could be cool with their being gay. I just figured it was shameful in every family." He continued, "It was all so liberating, because what it really meant was that I didn't have to be alone, and that accepting help and encouragement from other people was a good thing. It gave me an unbelievable sense of freedom, because I could draw on the combined strength of the group."

Today, Kent is out of the closet, successful, and working in his chosen profession of pharmacology at one of the top medical centers in Los Angeles. "When I first started graduate school, I thought maybe I made the decision to study pharmacology because of my parents. And for a while, I reevaluated my decision to go into this field. But after I opened myself up to the possibility that I might have made a mistake, I actually discovered that I loved my classes and the field. I've never regretted my career choice, but I'll tell you that without the personal support of my gay friends, I never would've made it. I like to think I'm where I am today because of other people, not because I avoided them."

Accepting Daily Success

Recognizing, accepting, and appreciating your road to success actually facilitates the achievement of your long-term professional goals. Here are five steps I encourage people to implement in their daily lives in order to feel good about accepting success in the present.

1. Right now, affirm for yourself that incredible career opportunities exist today for everyone in the gay community. There are workplaces where it's possible to be valued and rewarded for your talents and skills, and not held back because of sexual orientation.

2. Talk about your career plans with someone else. When you articulate what it is you want to do and where you want to go, it becomes real and it becomes yours. When it's real, it's achievable.

3. Spend five minutes at the end of each day envisioning your perfect job and your perfect life. If you can't see where you're going in your mind's eye, it's difficult to get there. If you feel you should be further along in your career, remember that those feelings are reflective of the human condition in general—everyone thinks they should be more accomplished. It's okay not to be at your final destination today. Think of it this way: if you were already there, you would have no reason for improving and growing, and no incentive to achieve.

4. Take steps toward improving your health and appearance. Maybe that means taking the stairs instead of the elevator, or having a salad instead of a burger and fries at lunch. It will improve the quality of your life as well as your outlook, which positively impacts your career. Why? Because you're doing something for you. It works!

5. Find something to laugh about, whether it's your favorite episode of a television sitcom that you've taped or your neighbor's unbelievably bad comb-over! It really doesn't matter what you're laughing about, as long as you're laughing.

Allowing Change to Impact Your Career

As human beings, we cannot escape the effects of change. This reality factors into your professional life because it means that you continually have new reference points to consider when making career decisions. In fact, change makes it impossible for you to create a single career plan right after college and expect it to meet your needs for the next fifty years. As a career development tool, the Seven Points of Success will always reflect these changes, because built into its design is your ability to redefine your unique identity and the workplace environment relative to new reference points along your lavender road to success.

The first few years of the twenty-first century have dramatically confirmed how world events immediately impact the world of work. After the events of 9/11, my interviews provoked a great deal of discussion about how the external world can change within seconds, and the dramatic impact that world events can have on individual careers. Several people I spoke with had family or friends who lost loved ones and colleagues in the attack on the World Trade Center. In the words of one woman whose cousin escaped death but not injury, "Gay or straight, this type of irrational violence does not discriminate."

TALKING ABOUT . . . EXTERNAL CHANGES

Lydia, a forty-year-old accountant in Laguna Beach, California, experienced a profound reaction as a result of the horrendous events of 9/11. We spoke early on a Saturday morning, and since it turned out that we live near each other, we decided to meet for coffee. She told me, "At some point on 9/11, while watching all of the devastation on television, I found myself wondering how many people died that day who were just like me, women and men who rode up in the elevators every day, saying hello to friends and co-workers, but never letting anyone know who they really were because they were gay."

Up until this point in her life, Lydia had never been out of the closet in any of her workplaces. "For the most part, if I needed to forsake my own identity and pretend to be straight for the sake of my job, then I became the straightest woman on earth while I was at work." But that was about to change. "Nothing has ever affected me more than 9/11," she said.

I asked her if there was one thing that she could identify that caused her to change the way she thought about how she wanted to live her professional life. Her answer was simple and honest. "For several days after the attack on the World Trade Center, I couldn't stop watching television. Even at work, no one did anything except watch the news. One morning, a woman appeared on the screen who looked exactly like my mother. She was small and frail, and was holding a picture of her daughter. She was asking anyone and everyone if they had seen her daughter in all the chaos. I fell apart, and barely managed to get back to my office before bursting into tears. I knew that if I had been in one of the towers, my own mother would be down there at ground zero, doing the exact same thing. The look on that woman's face haunts me to this day. Then, I had this crazy and inappropriate thought. What if it had been me? Would people somehow find out after my death that I was a lesbian? That single thought changed how I approach my life. I was enraged that such a stupid and insignificant thought was even part of my consciousness, and that I gave homophobic bigotry any value whatsoever after what had just happened to thousands of families. The fact that my sexual orientation was something I would want to hide—even in death—was a wake-up call that something had to change. Suddenly, the people I worked with who would think less of me because I was a lesbian seemed insignificant to my life." I asked her what she meant by the word "insignificant." She said, "It's simple. Life is too precious and too short to spend more than half of your waking hours with bigotry. I didn't realize how much my own homophobia had affected the way I lived my life until that day, and that it was taking a toll on my career." She told me, "You'll never feel free until you break away from people who want you to be someone you're not. Indulging their homophobia won't bring you success. I tried it, and it failed." The following summer, Lydia left her job as an accountant with a national telecommunications company and joined the finance department at a major California state university. In her new position she's out of the closet and valued for her own individuality. "This is the first job I've ever had that makes me feel good about myself. It's also the first time I've actually looked forward to going to work, and I attribute those positive changes to freedom. It's like getting out of prison after being put there on false charges."

The sooner you take over the process of defining who you are, and how important and valuable you are, the sooner you'll achieve your own lavender success.

Adding Value to Your Journey

Enjoying your road to success doesn't require that your own needs be the focus of your entire journey. Helping others in the gay community become successful requires some conscious effort, and involves crossing gender, racial, economic, and geographical borders. Taking the time to help strengthen the professional standing of others—and not just within the gay community, but within all minority communities—besides being the right thing to do, strengthens who you are in the world and enhances your own success.

Margaret Mead once said, "Never doubt that a small group of thoughtful, committed citizens can change the world. Indeed, it's the only thing that ever has." The empowerment that you'll gain when you help someone else professionally, whether by providing a networking contact, passing along information about a job opportunity, or sharing wisdom about your field or industry, will *When you strengthen yourself and others, you are achieving.* add fuel to your own engine. Real success is built on the belief that you have the authority to achieve. That belief is the hallmark of career empowerment, and a key to giving yourself the gift of enjoying your lavender road to success.

ACHIEVING YOUR DREAMS AS YOURSELF

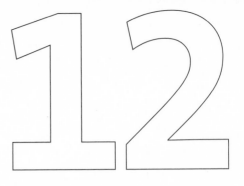

Overcoming Lavender Discrimination

A FEW WEEKS PRIOR TO BEGINNING WORK on this chapter I attended a play based on Barbara Ehrenreich's wonderful book *Nickel and Dimed* in downtown Los Angeles. Her work uncovers the daunting struggle that millions of Americans with low-paying jobs face each day simply trying to get by. That evening, along with two colleagues from the university, I sat in my cushy theater seat and watched real stories about women and men all across the country who are trapped in abusive workplaces. Watching the play, I became painfully aware of a truth that the people represented on the stage shared with gay people employed in homophobic environments. When people are faced with workplace subjugation, whether it's due to lack of opportunities or sexual orientation, often the only thing that keeps them going is fear.

During the second phase of my research, I found that many gay people have endured appalling treatment at some point in their careers because they felt their sexual orientation rendered them unemployable. Several people told me that they felt less deserving of respect and equality in their professional lives because they're gay, which is ultimately what kept them in abusive workplace environments. In other words, the internal dialogue goes like this: "No matter what type of job you offer me, and no matter how badly you treat me, I'll take it, because that's all I'm worth." That thought pattern is a lie. You deserve the same opportunities, salary, and respect that's afforded every other hardworking person in the workforce. You have the right to be treated with dignity in the workplace and have the opportunity to succeed.

I found that, for some people, an abusive professional setting can actually become comfortable. One person told me, "It was easier to believe my employer was the sole reason for my career woes than it was to take action and make changes." How many times have you thought, "It's not me, it's them—it's their problem." The dilemma of this statement is that when you work in an environment that's intimidating, unfriendly, or even hostile, it becomes your problem because it's part of your everyday life. Regardless of how the unjust circumstances came about, you have to work to overcome oppressive and discriminatory environments and create the success you deserve.

Your success isn't up to "them," it's up to you.

Empowering Yourself with Knowledge

As we've already discussed, 29 percent of the survey respondents reported that at some point they have experienced verbal or physical abuse in the workplace because they are gay. Selisse Berry, the executive director of Out & Equal Workplace Advocates, told me that as a result of my findings and other recent studies that mirror these statistics it's clear that gay people continue to face harassment, hostility, and discrimination. "Most people don't realize that we can be fired in most states just because of our sexual orientation. Change needs to happen on many levels. And it's imperative for workplaces to enact polices that will protect the LGBT community from discrimination to ensure a place that is safe for all employees."

Let's take a current snapshot of reality for gay Americans in the workplace. At the time of publication, only Washington, D.C., and the following fourteen states outlaw employment discrimination based on sexual orientation:

California	New Hampshire
Connecticut	New Jersey
Hawaii	New Mexico
Maryland	New York
Massachusetts	Rhode Island
Minnesota	Vermont
Nevada	Wisconsin

What does this list mean for you as a gay person in the national work-force? In every state not on this list you can be discriminated against, harassed, or fired because of your sexual orientation. With that rather sobering fact on the table, keep in mind that employers who protect gay workers from discrimination do exist in states not on that list. Therefore, as you move forward in your career and make decisions about where to work, if there is no state law in place that protects you against discrimination as a member of the gay community, you need to pay even greater attention to the internal reality of an organization.

TALKING ABOUT . . . DISCRIMINATION AND HARASSMENT

For the last two years Gianni has worked for a well-known cable television network in New York City, successfully writing and producing programs about financial issues. At thirty-three, he's placed himself in a company with a diverse workplace environment that provides members of the gay community the same opportunity to succeed as everyone else. However, before landing his current position, he struggled for three years at a financial magazine, also in New York City, where he was harassed and denied assignments because he's gay and out of the closet. "The atmosphere at the magazine is conservative and exclusive, like an upscale old-boys' club in Manhattan. Even though who they are didn't bother me, it didn't take long to find out that I sure bothered them." He said, "I was never physically threatened or assaulted, because in New York City, at least, I did have rights. But if it weren't for local, not state, laws at the time, I'm sure there would've been problems beyond what actually happened."

Gianni told me that the first year on the job was the most difficult, but as time passed it became easier to accept the discrimination at work. "It's a terrible thing to become numb to abuse, but that's exactly what happened." He continued, "More than anything else, it was about the conservative hetero-financial types making sure I knew I wasn't part of their group because I was gay." It was also clear that they wanted to make Gianni feel as bad as possible about himself. When I asked him why he stayed for three years, he said, "Because I wanted to have the name of the magazine on my resume. And for a while, I was getting to do some interesting stories. So I felt the trade-off was worth it. But when it became clear that I was really good at what I do and I was getting outside recognition, the premium assignments started to dry up."

I asked him about the type of behaviors that took place. "Every so often, this 'in-group'—all men and all over thirty-five—would get together in the office next to mine and make sure I heard the word 'fag' every so often as part of their conversation. And whenever they said it, they always burst out laughing like it was the punch line to a joke." He told me that more frequently he heard negative comments about people they thought were gay. "Sometimes the tone they used was almost violent, like all this hate was just bubbling below the surface looking to get out. I was never part of those conversations, but they always happened when I was close enough to hear them."

When you take control of your professional destiny, you empower yourself to make career decisions that benefit you.

After two and a half years with the magazine, Gianni said that the "in-group's" most homophobic member was promoted to senior editor. "I think my being out really pushed his buttons. Once he was appointed to take over as my editor I knew it was time to get out. Ironically, his promotion actually focused me on my own career. I made the decision not to wait around for things to change. It was time to leave, and it was the best career decision I've ever made."

Identifying the Source

Subtle and often unexpected disparaging comments from coworkers, clients, and bosses happen more often than overt acts of hostility or aggression. And although all acts of discrimination negatively impact the workplace environment for members of the gay community, it's nonetheless important to identify the type of discrimination you're facing in order to better understand how it affects you and your career. Based on my research, I found that the various types of discrimination that occur in the workplace against the gay community fall into five categories:

- Offensive language. Single or occasional instances of antigay verbal references in the form of innuendo, jokes, or personal opinion statements that demean any member of the gay community because of their sexual orientation

- **Offensive materials.** Single or occasional instances of the posting in public or private workplace spaces of antigay notes, newspaper articles, flyers, or religious slogans or items that demean any member of the gay community

- **Persistent harassment.** Ongoing acts of antigay behavior, including offensive language, jokes, or the posting of antigay materials, that seeks to demean any member of the gay community

- **Overt hostility.** Any act or event that is meant to threaten, intimidate, or discriminate against any member of the gay community because of their sexual orientation, whether it's a single occurrence or on an ongoing basis

- **Severe aggression.** Any act or event that jeopardizes the physical safety or mental well-being of any member of the gay community because of their sexual orientation

TALKING ABOUT . . . "DISGUISED" DISCRIMINATION

Midway through my research I was asked to speak about the issue of sexual orientation in the workplace at a luncheon attended by leaders and members of minority employee groups representing several major Southern California companies. Emily, one of the other speakers on the panel, made a powerful presentation about how humor can sometimes mask discrimination in the workplace. She began her presentation by talking about her own identity as a straight Hispanic woman in her early forties. Hispanics represent more than one thousand employees in her company.

Language is powerful. It can evoke every human emotion from love to hate.

Emily said that early in her career, she would remain silent about anti-Hispanic remarks. She told us that at one point in her career she worked for a man who continually made negative comments about every minority community under the sun, but always ended each remark with, "Oh, I'm just joking." Emily said that she justified her inaction by telling herself that his jokes didn't really matter because no one respected him anyway. She said, "When I look back, I realize that all of those comments did a lot of damage to my self-image and the self-image of others." She concluded her presentation with a very candid summary. "Looking at it another way, not making any noise about what was going on was the equivalent of accepting his bigoted jokes and remarks as valid. If you have a platform to change the environment for the better because your company has inclusive policies, put your network in place and work with other people in the company who condemn bigotry to do your best to make your workplace equal for everyone."

Measuring the Level of Offense

In most cases, I found that for acts falling into the offensive language or offensive materials categories, there was a measurable difference in the level of offense based on the relationship with the offender. For example, if the person who said or did something offensive was a friend or a colleague viewed as gay-friendly, the act was generally overlooked. If it came from someone who was new, disliked, or known to be homophobic, the exact same behavior was considered much more offensive. Should it be? Probably not, because each offensive remark or material is still an act of discrimination. But situational context and the history of the relationship make a difference. However, don't forget that your relationship history will also make it easier to remind someone to choose their words more carefully.

TALKING ABOUT . . . THE OFFENDER

Cynthia is forty-two and works for an inclusive technology company with several out-of-the-closet employees in upper-management positions. Cynthia is also out of the closet and successful in her role as an accounting manager. "I never thought that as an out gay woman I would enable a discriminatory work environment, but that's exactly what I did for several years." When Cynthia joined the company almost six years ago, she reported to a man who professed to be an advocate of diversity but who actually sounded like, in her words, a "redneck bigot." She said, "He made terrible off-the-cuff remarks about women, gays, and people of color, often to people's faces. But because he always appeared to be supportive of minorities within our department, I defended him to the hilt to other people in the company. I'd always point out that he had promoted several minority employees, so how much of a bigot could he be?" Cynthia also told me that on several occasions her boss's comments would bring people to tears. She defended him even then, telling her coworkers to look at his actions more than his words.

Cynthia said that over the course of several years numerous employees made formal complaints without any resolution. One day a particularly bad incident occurred during which he ridiculed an employee's right to visit a nearby synagogue on her lunch hour. Cynthia told her boss privately that he'd be advised to keep his remarks behind closed doors because it was causing low morale and unhappiness in the office. How did he respond to her suggestion? "He didn't like it at all. In fact, he was furious."

Even jokes can hurt when they demean who you are as a human being.

On that day Cynthia saw something in her boss's eyes that made her realize there was some truth behind his so-called wit. I asked her how this changed the relationship. She said, "It was never the same, although it was never discussed."

Cynthia's boss finally left the company and moved into a higher position with a competitor across town. Subsequently, she was promoted into his position. "The real reason he left was because he'd become totally isolated within the company. No one wanted to work with him or even speak to him. There are so many workplaces out there that are losing money and time because of inappropriate behavior."

I was curious about how she now got along with those employees who had suffered under his leadership. "I've tried to make up for it, maybe too much. I feel guilty for sticking up for him for so long, but he caused a lot of damage. If I ever find myself in that situation again, there's no way I'll allow destructive behavior to take place when it demeans other people and holds them back. If it makes someone else feel bad, it's no joke."

EXERCISE **Is Lavender Discrimination Standing in the Way of Your Success?**

In order to determine whether a barrier exists in your workplace stemming from lavender discrimination, it's necessary to assess the overall climate.

1. Take a blank sheet of paper and divide it into five columns. Label each column in the following order, using the five categories of discrimination already outlined in this chapter:

   • Offensive Language
   • Offensive Materials

- Persistent Harassment
- Overt Hostility
- Severe Aggression

2. Next, write down any act or event that falls into one of these categories under the appropriate heading. Also write down the dates and the name of the offender.

3. Rank each event on a scale of one to five according to the degree to which it was unacceptable to you. If an event really bothered you, rank it as a five. If it barely registered on your radar, rank it as a one.

4. Using a highlighter, mark those acts that went unchecked. In other words, if the offender didn't get called out by anyone for his or her behavior, highlight it.

5. Assess the number of threes, fours, and fives in your workplace environment. Do you have a fairly lengthy list? Are the majority of these events also highlighted?

6. Finally, ask yourself if these behaviors are coming from just one person or whether there are multiple offenders? If it's just one person, consider the level of that person's authority. In a small company, for example, if the offender is also the owner there's little chance that he or she will be held accountable, unless local or state laws protect you against discrimination based on sexual orientation. On the other hand, if there's a mechanism in place within the company to correct the situation, then there's a greater likelihood that positive change can take place.

Turning Oppressive Myths into New Truths

At the beginning of this chapter I mentioned just a few of the barriers that people in the study cited as reasons they remained working in an environment where homophobic coworkers, clients, or bosses were obstacles that stood in the way of their success. Let's address the principles on which these oppressive environments are based, and then take away their power by exposing them as myths.

● ● ●

Myth #1: No other employer will hire you because of your sexual orientation.

New Truth: Your sexual orientation is not an obstacle because there are employers in all fields that will value who you are as an individual. These employers do not make hiring decisions based on race, gender, socioeconomic background, or sexual orientation. Affirm this for yourself by going to the Human

When you replace outdated and oppressive myths with new truths, you strengthen your own role in the career decision-making process.

Rights Campaign website at www.hrc.org and the websites of many of the organizations listed in the back of this book and familiarize yourself with all of the companies that have already included you within their mission.

• • •

Myth #2: You are less deserving of respect and equality at work because you're gay.

New Truth: It is a basic human right to be given an equal chance to succeed based on your talent and abilities. Bigots all over the world count on minority communities to buy into this myth in order to keep them down. Reject it and throw it away. If you feel you need a symbolic ritual, write this myth on the bottom half of a piece of paper along with your new truth on the top half. Cut the piece of paper in two, dividing the myth from the new truth. Now shred the myth into hundreds of small pieces until no letter can be recognized and throw it away. It doesn't deserve a second more of your time.

• • •

Myth #3: It's okay to endure a troubled professional setting because it has become comfortable.

New Truth: Although an abusive environment can become familiar, you'll pay a high price for staying there. You can find a new environment where you'll be valued and successful.

• • •

Myth #4: If you leave a job too soon, it will look bad on your resume.

New Truth: If you leave a job because of discrimination or harassment, potential new employers who value a diverse workforce will not penalize you for leaving. In other words, you shouldn't be cast as a job hopper or troublemaker. It's perfectly acceptable to make professional changes when you are being harassed at work. Remember, however, that dealing honestly with the situation doesn't mean spending the entire interview talking about your traumatic past. Reframe your negative experience and make your own diversity a strength by addressing how much you value this potential new employer's commitment to a diverse workforce.

Surviving While You Plan Your Exit

It's much easier to survive day to day when you know it's a temporary situation. One of my first interviews was with Kyle, a thirty-six-year-old administrator at a major regional museum. He told me that he knew his current position had no long-term value because, after four years, there was no place for him to advance except into his boss's job. He also said there were no long-term professional benefits to realize if he stayed. Kyle told me that his boss was gay-friendly but ineffective, and he didn't recognize the contributions of others, regardless of who they were. Kyle called him an "equal opportunity exploiter."

Kyle likened his job to a head cold. "If you thought it was going to last forever you'd jump off the nearest and tallest bridge." I asked him if he would then liken himself to someone who was simply taking antihistamines to make the discomfort bearable, or if he was more like the cold sufferer who made plans to get more rest, eat better, and take vitamins to try and prevent it from happening again?

What's the difference between the two? The first example is passive; the second one is proactive. When you find yourself in a workplace environment that doesn't allow you to succeed because you're gay, the first decision you need to make is that it is a temporary situation, and that you have the authority to move forward. Without that acknowledgment, it's almost impossible to find the energy to create an exit plan—and creating an exit plan is the most empowering and proactive approach toward overcoming an oppressive environment.

EXERCISE **Creating an Exit Plan**

Making the decision to leave a job because you're not allowed to succeed takes courage, determination, and an effective plan. The following seven steps will help you make a successful transition into a workplace where you can be respected for who you are and prosper as a professional.

1. Recognize that you will never be treated fairly in a workplace that discriminates based on sexual orientation. Don't make excuses or procrastinate. The time to move forward is now!

2. Network with other gay professionals in your field who are out of the closet at work. Networking will provide you with necessary emotional support and proof that it's possible to be valued at work for who you are, and not treated as an outcast because you're gay. Ask yourself this question: are there gay people in my field who are out of the closet and successfully doing what I want to do? I promise you the answer to that question is yes. Never forget that if other people can do it, so can you.

3. Develop your resume and focus on your accomplishments. Writing your resume is a self-affirming act that signals you're going to make a move.

4. Repeat step 1.

5. Identify and apply for new jobs in diverse organizations that provide gay employees with an equal chance to succeed. The positive experiences of your peers described throughout this book confirm that you can find a workplace that provides a level playing field in virtually all industries.

6. Check in with your networking contacts from step 2. You'll find encouragement, assistance, and a sense of community that will give you the energy and motivation to make positive changes.

7. Prepare for all interviews and negotiate a fair salary and benefits package. The key is doing your research. Being prepared leads to confidence. Confidence leads to success. You'll find specific tips for interviewing and negotiating an offer in chapter 10. In the "Resources" section in the back of the book, you'll find websites that provide information to help you research companies and salaries.

Finding the courage to move forward and feel good about who you are in the world is almost impossible unless you first affirm your right to achieve in a workplace that's free of bigotry, discrimination, and harassment. It's critical to your own emotional well-being to align yourself with an employer who deserves your talents and skills. If you're in a negative environment, you'll find that survival becomes more manageable when you're engaged in the process of planning your exit. Knowing that you're being proactive will give you the energy and resiliency to make a positive change. Remember that there are no professional rewards for being a martyr, so don't get stuck in a bad situation because of fear or self-doubt.

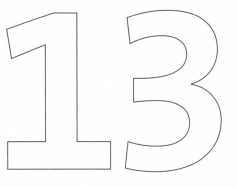

Creating Your Own Equality

THE FIRST TIME I REFLECTED ON WHAT it really meant to be "tolerant" of someone's sexual orientation was several years ago when I visited a friend with a broken leg. When I asked her how she was getting along, she rolled her eyes and said, "I'm tolerating it." A few days later, I was reading an article about a straight actor portraying a gay character and found myself uncomfortable with how the word "tolerant" was being used. The actor adamantly professed his heterosexuality, and then

Success isn't possible in a company where you're thought of as an inconvenience.

said, "but I'm completely tolerant of gay people." The word glared at me. I immediately thought of my friend with a broken leg. For her, being tolerant was putting up with an irritating inconvenience, enduring a burden that she couldn't wait to get rid of as quickly as possible.

Several people I interviewed told me that in their opinion, even the word *acceptance* doesn't represent the ideal, because acceptance suggests doubt about one's worthiness. Instead, people hoped for unqualified equality, meaning that sexual orientation and gender identity would have no professional relevance. Are we there? No, and we're not even close. However, understanding what the ideal looks like and how to achieve a reasonable facsimile in the here and now can inspire and guide us as a community to work toward that perfect state of *unqualified equality*.

Becoming the Best at What You Do

Minority communities understand that in today's working world there's a need to work harder than your colleagues and outperform them just to be considered "as good". For the gay community, the less an employer is committed to gay diversity, the more you're going to have to prove yourself in the workplace.

On the subject of working harder to be accepted, entrepreneur and philanthropist Tim Gill told me, "In some ways, I think the fact that gay people feel looked down on can inspire them to try even harder to prove themselves. Basically, if you're a stellar performer, people will be less concerned about your social life." He continued, "I think some people's response to the societal stigma [of being gay] is to retreat—

Being tolerated because of your sexual orientation suggests that being gay is an inadequate state of being—and you deserve more.

to work at jobs where they don't have the responsibilities or the exposure to be scrutinized." Tim shared an interesting hypothesis he attributed to a friend, who made the following observation: "There are very few mediocre gay people. They either excel at what they do, or they just retreat and don't try."

TALKING ABOUT . . . BEING THE BEST

Ben, a twenty-eight-year-old accountant in Los Angeles, California, with one of the "big four" accounting firms said that although his boss was gay-friendly, several colleagues in his office were not. He recently had the opportunity to successfully change his immediate work group for the better.

He described the events leading up to the turnaround. During the busy tax season, he was assigned to work closely with two of his less-than-friendly colleagues, one male in his fifties and one female in her forties. "We were working on an audit that was particularly difficult, and we took turns working weekends. As we were coming down to the wire, my male colleague had an unexpected family event and needed to go out of town. I knew it meant a lot to him to be able to go, so I went the extra mile and offered to cover for him—even though at the time, I knew he wouldn't have done the same for me. That was a turning point in our relationship. I also found a huge error that weekend that had been made by another group, which prevented all of us from getting nailed. If I had to say what changed, it would be that he saw me in a different light after that weekend. Now he's always telling me I'm a 'damn good accountant.' Before that, I'd say he just saw me as the gay guy at work."

Ben told me that he believed the turnaround was possible due to the company's inclusive policies for its gay employees and because his boss had always been supportive. He said that he doubted he would've had a chance to change anyone's opinion about his professional value without these policies.

Your "Equality Equation"

Ben's experience demonstrates the importance of being visible as a gay man at a company with inclusive policies that give value to his unique identity. In addition, he took action by going above the call of duty when he offered to work an extra weekend, demonstrating his commitment to his job and his colleagues. In addition, his talents and skills factored into his success when he found an error, and his stellar performance helped his entire group avoid a costly mistake. Your potential to succeed, then, can be seen as a result of adding up these factors.

VISIBILITY + COMPANY SUPPORT + ACTION +
TALENTS AND SKILLS + STELLAR PERFORMANCE
= YOUR EQUALITY

Committing to Diversity as a Societal Goal

Creating a workplace dedicated to equality requires that everyone who believes in the value of a diverse workforce remains focused on making positive changes. Some changes are made in individual workplaces. Other changes are more far-reaching. In 2002, for example, even in the midst of a very conservative political climate, overwhelming ballot victories in many states across the country affirmed and supported equal rights in the workplace for the gay community. Both types of change were made possible by the dedication and commitment of gay and straight people alike who believe in unqualified equality and creating environments that foster positive change.

TALKING ABOUT . . . DOING THE RIGHT THING

Jeri is a thirty-two-year-old executive with a national telecommunications company in Thousand Oaks, California. During an interview for a promotion, she was told by her boss that if she got the job, she would need to remove her commitment ring when meeting with "certain large clients." Jeri and I met on campus to talk about her experience. She was eager to share her story and began to fill me in on the details as soon as we ordered lunch. After Jeri had spent three years as a top producer and being completely out of the closet at work, her regional vice president told her during an interview for a promotion that she would no longer have the same freedom in a new role.

Each step you take in becoming visible contributes to a more level playing field for the entire gay community.

Jeri is confident in her professional abilities and extremely comfortable with who she is. "When 'Mr. B.' said this to me, my ears didn't want to send the message to my brain. First of all, I'm thinking to myself, how illegal it is to tell me this in the state of California. Second, the irony was totally amazing. At a sales meeting earlier that same day he had talked ad nauseam about his commitment to honesty and integrity." She shook her head as she continued. "He couldn't even look at me when he told me I had to go back into the closet to get the promotion. He knew he was a hypocrite." Jeri said her boss explained himself by saying that if "certain business leaders" that she would be interacting with in the new job found out she was a lesbian, they'd jump ship to another company. Taking off her commitment ring before meetings became a condition of the promotion.

After Jeri told her boss that she would not remove her ring or go into the closet, someone else who was much less qualified was hired into the job. "Even beyond the discrimination, it was a personal slap in my face for not doing as he asked. In part, I also believe he made his hiring decision based on what would piss me off the most because I defied him. That's how he manages—out of spite."

Unwilling to accept the situation, Jeri filed an internal complaint. "Filing the complaint was a difficult decision for me. Even though the company provided me with the opportunity to challenge the appropriateness of his behavior, I came very close to just leaving the company." I asked if there was a defining moment that made her decide to stay and fight. She nodded her head yes. "A member of our gay employee resource group came to me and said he and his partner were having a commitment ceremony, and he asked me if I thought he should take his ring off before coming to work. That was it. I knew then and there I had to challenge the situation."

Jeri then began to thoughtfully and professionally gain the support of several top managers within the company. In the course of the investigation, it turned out Mr. B. had sent an email to another senior executive saying, "I can't jeopardize a multimillion-dollar account with a lesbian account executive." After several months of inquiry by the company's diversity officials, Jeri received her promotion along with a written letter of apology, reaffirming the company's commitment to providing equal opportunities for its gay employees. Soon after, Jeri said that Mr. B. resigned and took a new job with another telecommunications company. "He's been around a long time and his own network paid off. I try not to spend time thinking about him because I won that round. Actually, we all won."

As we finished lunch, I asked her what advice she'd give to others facing the decision whether to stay or look for another job. "The first order of business is to make sure that company policies and antidiscrimination laws allow you to have an equal voice. If you're in a one-horse town, so to speak, where your boss is the antigay mayor, antigay sheriff, and antigay jury and judge, then you don't have a chance. In that case, no matter what evidence you have, you're never going to win. In my case, I was fortunate because the opposite was true. But beyond that, you have to believe that what you're doing is the only 'right' thing to do. And that has to be more important than winning because the good guy doesn't always win." As we finished our lunch, she shared her final wisdom on the subject. "When you really believe that what you're doing is the right thing, and you have the moral conviction that goes along with your belief, you gain the power to win. And when you're true to yourself and your beliefs, you can't lose."

Identifying Yourself as an Achiever

A strong work ethic is beyond criticism. It's also the foundation for gaining positive recognition. In smart organizations, steps are taken to make sure that employees who are working harder and more effectively than the rest are rewarded.

Being recognized as an achiever provides you with a double benefit. Not only will you gain visibility, but your enhanced value will break down professional barriers, which will ultimately pave the way for greater individual success. It's analogous to running ahead and opening the door for yourself. When you're there and ready to go through, you won't have to slow down and open it.

Now here's the caveat. If your workplace environment is rampant with homophobia and the three "isms"—ageism, racism, and sexism—no matter how hard you work, you'll never be recognized in any way other than as the gay person at work. Gaining recognition as a standout employee who's valued and respected can only be achieved in an organization that provides you with the opportunity to succeed based on your unique identity.

TALKING ABOUT . . . DISCRIMINATION AND ACHIEVEMENT

Dimitri is a thirty-year-old portfolio manager in Los Angeles working with high–net worth individuals at a small, prestigious firm. He's been there for three years, following a difficult employment period at another Los Angeles firm, where he was not valued because he's gay. "After college, I put in my three years with a big banking firm that was just so-so in terms of being gay-friendly. But I did a good job and made great contacts. From there, I decided to pursue more hands-on investment work where I'd have the opportunity to work directly with clients. I thought I'd found a great company and blindly took the job without ever thinking about whether it was gay-friendly. I guess I just assumed it was like the large firm I came from— as long as you did your job, no one really bothered you, although they didn't want you to talk about being gay. But this place was a complete nightmare." Dimitri told me that it was made clear to him within the first month that being gay wasn't acceptable to the powers that be. He was told it would be in his best interests to play it straight. "I didn't like it, but I felt stuck and didn't want to job hop. So I stayed and paid."

Soon after he started the new job, Dimitri began dating a man who was employed in the same field, but with a firm that welcomed gay employees. As their relationship developed, so did Dimitri's awareness that his contributions at work weren't being valued in the same way as his new boyfriend's. "The harder I worked, the more shit I seemed to get from my boss. And once they knew for sure I was gay, although I never talked about it, they were out to get me." A year later, Dimitri decided to leave. "It didn't make sense to me to devote any more time to a firm that dehumanized me as a man. Even if it meant having a job on my resume that only lasted a year, I had to leave."

While Dimitri was looking for another position, his boyfriend was recruited by another company, leaving his job open. "It was good timing, and I had the right qualifications to apply for the job. Plus, I knew for a fact it was cool to be gay and out." After an intensive interview process he was offered the job and accepted. "It was like a huge weight came off my back. I didn't realize it until I was out of my old job, but I had changed. And not in a good way. After a year of being in this terrible company I had stopped laughing, stopped dreaming, and stopped getting out into the world in the way I had before. I was much less involved in life."

Dimitri told me that in some ways, he was appreciative of the experience. "It taught me that I had the right to expect fair and equitable employers." I was curious to hear his thoughts on how the future landscape for gay people in his field might change. "I think that positive change will ultimately be about supply and demand. Once there are enough people—gay and straight—who oppose dehumanizing employment practices, companies will change. Let's face it, if there are no workers available to put up with that crap, employers will be forced to change based on that demand, or there will be no supply of labor. I think my generation and those behind us will make positive changes that give everyone an equal voice."

Cultivating an Inner Circle Network

Getting ahead in your career requires cultivating positive relationships with your colleagues. Today more than ever before you must be connected to other people in order to succeed. In forward-thinking companies, there is an increasing focus on developing cultures that rely on interpersonal communication to get the job done. Regardless of your field or industry, it's almost impossible to be successful when you're isolated. Cultivating a network of gay and gay-friendly supporters at work will keep you connected to the flow of information and also provide you with diversity advocates to keep workplace homophobia in check. Once assembled, your workplace network will provide you with three major career benefits:

- Access to formal and informal workplace communication. Without being connected to others, it's less likely that you'll be part of the workplace team. If you're not part of the team, information that might help you succeed in your job will not be forthcoming.

- Advocates to help prevent workplace homophobia. Straight colleagues who are gay-friendly and supportive can become effective at-large diversity educators, calling others on inappropriate or antigay language and behavior.

- A rich professional development resource for your own career advancement. Because your workplace network consists of people in your field, each person is a contact or even a potential mentor or future employer. They are invaluable links to professionals at other companies, and can also serve as solid professional references.

Identifying and Creating Your Network of Allies

The following five steps will help you create a trusted and valuable inner circle network of allies that will help you successfully navigate your workplace environment.

1. Identify gay colleagues at all levels within the organization and connect with them. Typical hierarchical barriers, which tend to prevent networking among employees at different levels, do not exist to the same extent when you are connecting with someone from your own community.

2. Take the time to listen and observe. A key element of putting together an effective inner-circle network is to include straight allies, and you need to figure out who's friendly and who isn't. Don't waste your time on anyone who exhibits signs of homophobic behavior: your inner circle is about assembling allies, not converting adversaries. At the risk of painting people with broad brushstrokes, you can often use how they spend their free time as a clue to how gay-friendly they are. Do they speak favorably about a television program with gay characters, or do they constantly quote the conservative host of a political talk show? Are they Democrats or Republicans? Yes, making assumptions based on these factors is generalizing, but there's no value in pretending that certain ideological beliefs are not generally associated with various societal clusters. It's a fact that you're going to find more antigay sentiment at the Republican National Convention than at the

Democratic National Convention. Certainly do your homework and base your opinions on fact, but also use your common sense.

3. Avoid gossips. If someone is talking about a colleague in a negative way or making fun of them, chances are he or she will do the same thing behind your back. Gossips usually don't have much clout in the workplace, either, so it's likely they won't provide you with any of the benefits you're seeking from your inner-circle network anyway.

4. Go slow. Have you ever met someone you thought was going to be your new best friend, only to have the relationship disintegrate as quickly as it began? Remember that it will be difficult, if not impossible, to avoid your colleague after things fall apart, so take the time necessary to develop quality relationships.

5. Provide in-kind support. Just like in your personal life, workplace relationships that benefit both parties will provide greater overall satisfaction and long-term benefits. When you support your workplace allies, you'll enhance your own success. The people who have been supported in their jobs will almost always return to their inner-circle network and help those people grow as well. So the more support you provide to the members of your network, the more support you'll receive in return.

• • •

Realizing a national workforce where isolation, harassment, and discrimination are extinct, and where enlightened people of all sexual orientations and genders believe that diversity makes the world a richer place to work and live in can be the goal to guide us. And we can all play a role in that evolution. Your voice may be loud, or you may make a quiet personal commitment. Both are vitally important. The cycle of bigotry and hatred is broken each day by people just like you. When you become visible, you chip away at bigotry, oppression, and intolerance. You'll be able to increase your own opportunities for success while enhancing your professional value. It doesn't matter what role you play, as long as you remember that you have the ability to change the world.

Contributing to Organizational Change

MAKING YOUR ORGANIZATION A BETTER place for gay people to work in is one of the best ways to keep moving forward along your own lavender road to success. Throughout the book, you've been introduced to many women and men who have enhanced gay diversity within their respective workplaces by utilizing existing gay-friendly policies and antidiscrimination laws. We know, of course, that not all of these employers were actually "walking the talk" of their equal employment opportunity statements. Still, when there are some policies in place to protect the rights of gay employees, you'll find that you have a greater opportunity to impact real organizational change.

I'm often asked whether it's possible to change the culture of an organization that's rooted in antigay sentiment, and my answer is always the same: "Any positive change that can be made is a step in the right direction." But remember, "positive change" within a homophobic workplace environment will not come soon enough to make it worth sacrificing your mind, body, and spirit—or your career.

The desire to be a catalyst for change, transforming your organization into a workplace that's equal for all people, is of course a professional virtue. However, I want you to consider that it's possible to be too virtuous. For example, being thorough is a valuable professional trait, but it's possible to be too thorough. If you overanalyze every project and interpersonal dynamic you encounter, create mountains of needless paperwork, and make ninety-minute presentations when you could easily make your point in half the time, being thorough is no longer a professional virtue, it's a liability.

If you've ever spent a great deal of time and energy on a project that doesn't yield positive results, you know firsthand how frustrating it feels. The same holds true when it comes to changing an organization that doesn't value doing the right thing.

You can choose when and where to invest your time and energy.

Yes, it's admirable to want to change the way closed-minded people think about who you are as a human being, but no, it isn't admirable to give up your own career in that pursuit.

When you're in an organization that has some type of gay-friendly policy, you have the ability to bring the internal reality of the organization closer to that policy without sacrificing your own career. In doing so, you'll also be contributing to the extinction of homophobic employers.

Simply put, embracing a diverse workplace is a necessity of twenty-first-century globalization, and if employers don't get that, they will eventually go out of business. If you have any doubt, take a look at the social and economic dynamics surrounding the fall of the Ming dynasty.

It's possible to improve opportunities for other gay people in the workplace and move forward in your own career.

The rulers decided they didn't need to include or do business with anyone they thought was an "outsider," and so they broke away from the rest of the world. Essentially, they deemed themselves superior to everyone else, much like the homophobic employers who may be affiliated with today's religious right. However, the Ming dynasty couldn't sustain their isolated economy, and their kingdom crumbled.

There's essentially no difference between the philosophy responsible for the fall of the Ming dynasty and the philosophy of bigoted employers who choose not to create inclusive workplace environments. History is overrun with examples of fallen countries, governments, and businesses that mirrored the dynamics of the Ming dynasty. In order to be successful and long-lived, an organization must embrace inclusiveness and diversity. Without them, innovation will never occur. Our global economy along with the evolution of society will leave these companies behind sooner rather than later. Align yourself with a company that's moving forward, not backward.

Increasing Your Effectiveness as a Workplace Role Model

When you set out to create change within an organization, you need to be able to convince others that change is a desirable thing, and that's where your credibility comes into play. In order to convince others that gay diversity is good business, it's necessary to be viewed as a workplace role model. Workplace role models, whose hallmark is professional excellence, exhibit three primary behaviors:

- They commit to their jobs and roles within the organization.

- They go above and beyond the call of duty to do consistently superior work.

- They support other employees by pitching in to help when appropriate.

If you practice these three behaviors within an organization that already has some type of gay-friendly policy in place, you'll have the opportunity to be heard and influence change. In those organizations that are just beginning to crack open the door to gay diversity, personal credibility will play an even greater role.

TALKING ABOUT . . . BEING EFFECTIVE

Emilio is a twenty-nine-year-old physician who's currently in his last year of residency at a Los Angeles hospital. On his survey, Emilio wrote a note telling me that he had recently helped start a group for gay employees at the hospital. Because a medical resident works extremely long hours, I was eager to find out about his process for establishing the group. When I spoke with him about his accomplishments, Emilio was still at the hospital going over patient records even though he was off duty. He told me, "I'd definitely say I'm the senior resident who spends the most time at the hospital. I love what I do and want to be the best doctor I can be." Emilio told me he's always felt the need to go "above and beyond" what's required of him because he's a double minority. "Being Latino and gay means I've got to prove myself twice as many times as straight white guys in order to be credible."

I asked him about his motivation for starting a gay employees group at the hospital. "From day one, I've had so much support, and there was a need to make that atmosphere more prevalent in other areas of the hospital. A more formal network for gay employees needed to happen." When I asked him if the hospital had any existing policies designed to protect gay employees, he didn't hesitate to honestly respond. "Overall, I'd rate the hospital as a six on a gay-friendly scale of one to ten. Even though the website says they don't discriminate based on sexual orientation, and I've personally never had a problem being out of the closet, I've heard homophobic remarks from other professional staff members. It varies a lot from department to department, and that's the main reason I wanted to start this group."

It makes fiscal sense to treat all employees with respect and dignity.

There was a specific incident that convinced him to start the group. "A friend of mine, who's also gay, wasn't even given the opportunity to interview for a promotion because a doctor in that particular group thought he was too effeminate. He needed an advocate, someone to stand up to people who think like that doctor and say, 'It's okay to be who you are as long as you do your job and do it well.' That's what the employee resource group is all about."

I asked Emilio how the hospital administration responded when they learned he was going to start the group. "There weren't any gasps or fainting, but there really wasn't anything they could do about it either because of their own policies. But I do know for a fact they weren't as worried about it as they might have been because of my own reputation. My attending physician even told an administrator, 'If Emilio's involved, it's going to be done right.' That made me feel like all the extra hours and time I've given to my job in the last two and a half years have paid off."

Educating Your Colleagues about the Value of Gay Diversity

In order to further develop the breadth and depth of gay diversity within your organization, it's important to educate colleagues and organizational leaders about how it will benefit them. There are three specific actions an organization needs to take to support gay diversity in the workplace:

- Provide a supportive and welcoming environment for gay employees
- Reach out specifically to gay customers and consumers
- Withdraw company philanthropic support from organizations that practice discrimination based on sexual orientation

In my role at the university I've had the opportunity to speak with hundreds of business leaders who represent all types of companies around the country about workplace diversity. When I bring up issues specifically related to gay diversity, I always ask the same questions:

- Do you reach out to potential employees from the gay community?

- Do you provide a safe environment for the gay women and men already at your company?

If the answer to both of these questions is yes, then I ask:

- Do you provide domestic partner benefits for your employees?

I'm pleased to report that in the past few years I've been told "yes" to each of these questions much more often than "no." The reason behind this trend is simple—it's good business to reach out to all potential customers and consumers, which of course includes the gay community. Educating the leaders of your organization about the financial benefits that can be realized from having a favorable corporate image within the gay community is a great place to start building your case.

In today's competitive business world, companies will have to reach out to all possible customers and consumers in order to remain viable. In fact, many gay-friendly employers listed in the Fortune 500 have told me that when it comes to the gay market share, creating a favorable image goes beyond advertising in *The Advocate* or *Out Magazine*. A favorable image originates with a company's reputation for how they treat their gay employees. In an era of instant communication, it's no longer possible to keep the truth about the internal reality of any organization a secret for too long. Today, when it comes to gay diversity in the workplace, the human resources function of any organization is directly connected to its advertising and public relations efforts. It's in every company's financial interest to generate a positive reputation among all minority communities, and in a connected society, word gets around fast.

Making the Case for Gay Diversity

When you advocate for gay diversity at work, it's essential to back up your position with facts. Being able to cite statistics and sources will give you the power to be heard loud and clear. Emphasizing the following five points will help you communicate the value of gay diversity to employers, and the websites listed below will give you invaluable and up-to-date information to back up these assertions.

- The gay market is valuable and loyal.

- Having a positive corporate image in the gay community can increase revenue.

- Reaching the gay market begins with inclusive internal policies and practices.

- The freedom for gay employees to be out in the workplace will add to overall productivity.

- Leading-edge companies already "get it."

The following websites will provide you with case studies, market share percentages, and estimates of money spent by gay consumers to support your message. It's a good idea to use case studies and the names of other companies that are most relevant to your field or industry. Remember that no smart leader wants the competitor to be the one setting trends or receiving favorable press because they are more inclusive. There's a great deal of value in using industry rivals who are doing a better job at gay diversity as a benchmark, and then showing your organization how to do an even better job. Present the problem and offer a solution.

www.hrc.org

www.glaad.org

www.glcensus.com

www.witeckcombs.com

www.commercialcloset.com

Influencing Change

Many people who have witnessed or influenced change within their own organizational culture told me that there's a strong correlation between mandated behavior and actual internal change. Mandated behavior, which some may term "politically correct" behavior, is regulated by an organization's equal employment opportunity statement, which may or may not include sexual orientation, or by regional laws that prevent discrimination and harassment. This is what prevents a homophobic coworker from calling you derogatory names or excluding you from company functions because you're gay. In other words, their behavior is forced upon them. But when people are "forced" to be nice to you to avoid losing their jobs or facing litigation, it can actually cause a shift in their attitudes and perceptions. A similar dynamic is at work when you tell someone you're feeling

Forced change can breed true enlightenment, and sometimes it's the only available approach.

great on a day that you're really not feeling so hot. By doing so you can avoid getting mired down in your own negativity and actually improve your outlook on life that day. This same energy can occur in the workplace. Some people won't change unless they are required to change. But in the process of required change, some people will actually "get it."

TALKING ABOUT . . . CHANGING COMPANY POLICIES

Todd is a thirty-five-year-old attorney in New York who utilized his law firm's own written policies on gay diversity to change the internal reality of his workplace environment. "Because I know the law and my employer knows the law, no one could publicly say or do anything at the office that might be interpreted as discriminatory or offensive to gay people because of our own equal opportunity statement. In fact, I was told that several people opposed including 'sexual orientation' in the statement when it was written several years prior to my joining the firm. Some of the senior partners are old-boy types, and their own personal philosophies didn't really reflect our employment policies." However, taking advantage of the firm's policies, Todd decided to strengthen the role of gay diversity within the organization. With the help of gay colleagues at other law firms, he formed a collective resource group with the specific purpose of recruiting new gay attorneys into their firms. "I knew a few of the senior partners at my firm hated the idea, but they couldn't do a damn thing about it because it wasn't in opposition to our hiring policies. In fact, it supported our policies."

Since joining the firm more than five years ago, Todd had put together his own inner-circle network within the firm, including a senior partner who has a gay son. "We have had many conversations about how the firm has ignored the need to recognize same-sex partnerships and provide benefits to partners, and I knew that he would support me on this issue with the power group." As a result of Todd's new resource group, he brought into his firm two heavily recruited new attorneys, and within a month three other employees came out of the closet. "It was wild. It seemed like all of a sudden being gay was the 'in' thing to do! There's a collective re-assurance that happens when you see more than one or two other people who are just like you." As for the senior partners who grumbled under their starched collars about his resource group, "They realized that having gay people at work didn't mean that their boardroom was going to be trans-formed into a disco." After several months Todd noted a gradual change within the organization as personal feelings started to more closely mirror the written policies. "This year, invitations to the holiday party actually included the names of same-sex partners. Half of the change I attribute to basic education through exposure, the other half to understanding that a diverse workforce is good for business. In the professional world, personal ability and delivery of the goods are the bottom line. I just forced them to walk the talk."

Leveraging Your Credibility and Likability

How many people can you name who always seem to get what they want because they're likable? Now, think of the term "likable" as meaning "people smart." It has very little to do with personality and a great deal to do with being aware of the sensitivities and trigger points of others. In a nutshell, a likable person is someone who knows what to say, when to say it, and how to say it.

Recently I was having lunch with a friend who was complaining about the approach his partner takes when pointing out his tendency to over-spend. "Instead of saying it in a way that will win me over to his side, he starts off by telling me that I'm exactly like his sister—a woman he knows I can't stand. Right then, I turn off and don't hear anything else he says because I'm so pissed off at being compared to his sister."

When you're aware of the types of messages people in your workplace are likely to respond to, you can get your message across in a way that has meaning. To a large extent, you just have to develop an awareness about what makes them happy and what makes them angry in terms of triggers. If you incorporate this awareness into your workplace communication, you'll immediately become someone who's likable, and you'll find yourself in the position to truly influence change.

Eliciting a real understanding of why enhancing gay diversity is the right choice for an organization requires the right message at the right time. In the previous section, Todd attributed 50 percent of his firm's change to "basic education through exposure." When you educate people about the value of providing a welcoming and inclusive workplace for the gay community, you simultaneously remove stigmas that exist in people's minds because they have a new understanding, or knowledge, about the gay community. Do you need to have

Combining likability with credibility gives you the opportunity to become a knowledge producer.

a certain type of personality to be a knowledge producer? Not at all. Everyone can be likable and credible at work. In fact, as I suggested in chapter 10, being gay provides you with "value-added" communication skills. Life itself has called upon you to be more insightful and aware of human emotions, and, in turn, more empathetic, than other people.

Becoming a Knowledge Producer

When you become a knowledge producer about the value of gay diversity in the workplace, the following five principles will ensure your credibility and keep your workplace communication functioning at a high level.

- Develop flexibility. No one responds to rigidity. Make sure you allow others to express their thoughts and respect their right to have them. Remember that in order to bridge what might be two very different worlds of thought, you have to first understand what that other world is thinking.

- Recognize that some people may have a negative opinion of you based on an illogical thought process. This will give you the ability to better target your own message in a way that will expose those thoughts as false. If you know what someone thinks about you based on preconceived ideas that have nothing to do with you, the better chance you have to expose those thoughts as inaccurate.

- Create rational dialogue on what can be a politically charged issue for some people. Diffuse irrational behavior with rational communication. Educating isn't preaching, so be careful not to shift your focus from creating new knowledge to defending who you are. When you heighten someone's understanding about the importance of gay diversity, you will also be supporting the gay community.

- Expose assumptions based on media stereotypes and right-wing propaganda. Recognize that some organizational leaders and colleagues will worry that your workplace will become a daily gay pride parade if they show too much support for gay diversity. Be sure to address these thoughts and talk about them. Provide the listener with a safe haven to talk honestly about their reservations. Once you know what their reservations are, you can expose unsound assumptions as nonissues. Don't forget that humor helps!

- Appropriately manage your visibility within the organization. It's not about being seen with the right people, it's about being seen with all people. Don't be someone who only networks with higher-ups, or only socializes with a certain group. Spread your excellence around! You will enhance both your credibility and likability when you're viewed as someone who appreciates and values a wide variety of personalities.

TALKING ABOUT . . . GETTING YOUR MESSAGE ACROSS

Just knowing that it's important to be aware of other people's emotions when communicating at work isn't enough. You have to put that knowledge into practice. Recognizing that your audience may be hearing about the gay community without any type of negative filter for the first time will help you effectively get your message across. Josh is a thirty-four-year-old project manager for a large construction company that's based in San Francisco. In his role, he's the main liaison between the company and the people on the job sites. He works closely with on-site construction crews, and, in his words, "construction crews aren't exactly known for being gay-friendly."

Josh is in a somewhat unusual situation for his field. The company he works for is headquartered in San Francisco and not only provides protection against discrimination and harassment for gay employees, but also offers domestic partner benefits. "Until last year, I was out of the closet to my boss and the people who work in the corporate office, but not to the crews I manage every day." At one point about a year into his tenure with the firm, Josh made a conscious decision to be closeted with his crew, because he felt being out would put him at a disadvantage as a manager.

"It's no secret this is a homophobic field. The guys on the crew are always calling each other 'fags' and 'queers'—and I figured my relationship with them would be ruined if they knew I was gay."

I asked him how he was able to keep his sexual orientation a secret from the crew, since he was out of the closet to his colleagues at the corporate office. He offered an interesting commentary on the division between blue- and white-collar workers in his field. "There's such a separation between the 'suits' and the workers. It's easy to be two people because rarely does either side communicate with the other except through people like me. We even have two holiday parties." Josh told me that, for the most part, the corporate office thinks of its employees on the construction sites simply as "labor." "Crews know that the front office people with MBAs don't think they have much to offer beyond their hands." He paused. "I thought that too until I came out to them."

After five years with the company, Josh had developed a reputation for being a superior project manager. "I knew my crew respected me, but I was very unsure about coming out." The catalyst that led him to come out was a conversation he overheard about a new member of the crew the others thought might be gay. "They were going on and on about having a 'fag' on their crew, and laughing about whose crotch he would grab first. One guy said, 'If he grabs me or even gets close to me, I'll take a hammer to his head.' I knew I had to speak out as a manager and a gay man." Josh told me that his first reaction to his crew's conversation was anger. "I got really pissed off thinking about how people could be so ignorant about what it really means to be gay. The fact that these guys automatically thought someone would be after them sexually just because he was gay was ludicrous to me. Still, I had to accept that it was a real thought for them."

The next day, Josh took his lunch break with several key members of the crew who participated in the previous day's conversation. "I decided to be completely honest and get a dialogue going on the subject. I wanted to take away as many negative misconceptions about being gay as possible and reiterate company policy. One of the guys asked me about my holiday plans and I thought, 'this is the perfect opening.' I didn't want it to be a big deal, so I tried to be as nonchalant as possible. I told them I was going to be with my partner's family, and made it sound as typical as their own plans." He noticed what he described as "a lot of shocked looks" going back and forth between the crew, and then there was an eternity of silence. "I thought my heart was going to jump out of my chest. Then, one of the guys said, "So, you're gay? We heard rumors about it, but we didn't want to believe them." Josh then answered all of their questions honestly, including, "Why do you want to be gay?"

"It's amazing to me how much people really don't know. Basic knowledge that I take for granted, like the fact that it's not a choice, it's just who I am, is totally new information. I think I did a lot of good, and it's a continual process. It wasn't like suddenly everyone was open-minded and nonjudgmental, but it took away some of their fear. I also reminded them that the company provides legal protection against discrimination for anyone that's gay." Josh said there was a definite change in the culture over the course of the next three months. "I attribute part of the improvement to the fact that there was no change in me and how I work with the crew. The first few days were a little tense, but now, no one cares much about whether I'm gay or straight. In fact, a couple guys have even asked if my partner and I had a good weekend, and I think that kind of dynamic will continue to become the norm. One guy on the crew even told me that he had a gay sister and told me how his mother, a devout Catholic, wouldn't speak to her. He asked me how he could get his mother to talk to his sister again."

How did it change his own career? "I feel like I'm a better supervisor because I'm being honest about who I am. I also feel like I'm completely free, and I've never felt that way before. It's like having power windows on your car after rolling them up and down for years. It's an amazing luxury that I'll never give up."

Becoming an Agent of Change

Many principles that will guide you on your lavender road to success can also empower you to be a catalyst for change. You'll always be more successful in influencing organizational culture and the dynamics of workplace communication when you're respected as a professional. The following seven steps will give you the ability to be an agent of change, making your organization a better place for gay employees and, therefore, yourself.

- Establish a reputation for being inclusive and receptive to change.

- Take a stand against all forms of bigotry and discrimination against all minority communities.

- Commit to doing excellent work and support your colleagues in the workplace.

- Participate in an existing gay employee group or, with the help of your inner-circle network, work to create one.

- Bring issues that promote workplace equality to the professional table.

- Advocate for more and better workplace policies that support gay employees and encourage the recruitment of gay job candidates.

- Hire and promote other qualified members of the gay community and support minority job candidates as you "walk the talk" of being committed to workplace diversity.

Standing Up for the Truth

Each person you've met in this chapter is an activist. Sometimes we think of activism as a behavior limited to the people in our community who appear on nightly news programs or lobby Congress for better and more inclusive laws. But the real definition is much broader. An activist is anyone who is part of the process of improving the world. Because each one of us can contribute to making the world and the workplace more equitable, we can all be activists. You have a unique contribution to make, and it will be invaluable because you're the only person in the world who can make it.

Activism is simply the act of standing up for the truth in a way that reflects your own unique identity.

When you live your life at work with honesty and integrity, you will be actively transforming the working world for yourself and all people who have been held back because of their sexual orientation or gender identity. Your influence may be quiet or it may be loud. At times, it may seem like no one is even listening, but I promise you it does make a difference, because *you* make a difference.

Success on Your Own Terms

THE ATTRIBUTES AND QUALITIES YOU ATTACH to the word *success* will decidedly affect how you approach your career. Defining what success means to you is an important step in the career development process that a lot of people overlook. Kelly, a longtime friend of mine, used to dream about becoming famous in the entertainment field. When we first met, her goal was simply to become a star. Over the course of the next ten years, from the age of twenty-five to thirty-five, she changed how she planned to become a star at least once a year. From actress to dancer to singer to model to stand-up comic, she was continually looking for a new job title that would provide her with stardom. On a video taken on her thirtieth birthday, someone asked her what she wanted out of life. She immediately replied, "Fame and money."

Focusing on the Importance of Your Unique Identity

Early in her career, Kelly defined achievement solely as the achievement of external rewards—in this case, fame and money. But fame and money are examples of career by-products, not evidence of achievement. Focusing on the by-products associated with a career will not necessarily contribute to your success. In other words, if you focus on the by-products of any career and not on the four points of your unique identity that create success—your individuality, talents, skills, and ego—it will be difficult to achieve your professional dreams.

Think of it like this. You can't be fame. You can't grow up to be money. When you focus on career by-products, you shift the focus from where it should be—on you—onto the external world. Does my friend Kelly have the talent to become a star that's also famous and rich? She sure does. But her early career decision-making process was flawed and delayed her achievement.

Kelly has always possessed a unique identity that empowers her to be a great actress. I've seen her transform herself on stage, making characters with personalities and traits that are completely opposite of her own so real that I'd completely forget it was her on stage. However, for those ten years she spent an equal amount of time pursuing all of the other professions I mentioned in search of fame and money.

On her fortieth birthday, I had the opportunity to ask her the same question someone else asked ten years earlier, "What do you want out of life?" This time her answer was remarkably different. She told me, "I'm focused on what I love, which is acting. I make a comfortable living in my profession and I've learned that I can define the word *star* in a way that has meaning for me." After more than a decade of being motivated by external images, Kelly is now achieving her dreams and discovering new ones based on her own identity. In the past few years she has also started to realize a substantial level of success as a television writer, again drawing from her own power source. When I ask her on her fiftieth birthday if she's still a star, I'm confident she'll tell me yes. And I have a feeling there will be a few Emmy Awards for writing on her mantel as well.

TALKING ABOUT . . . ACHIEVING SUCCESS

Janis is the corporate art director for a large multinational company in Southern California, and she is out of the closet at work as well as in her personal life. At thirty-four, she's achieved a level of success almost unheard of for someone her age. She has also come very close to losing everything she has worked for. After I received her survey along with some initial details about her experience, we set a time for an interview through an email exchange. At the end of her email, she wrote, "I've always been out, but I haven't always been open. I think a lot of lesbians and gay men are living the same way." I wasn't quite sure what she meant by "being out, but not open." Since we were planning to meet in just a few days, I decided to wait until we met in person to find out. It was the first question I asked when we sat down for lunch, and her answer offered a great deal of wisdom and insight about the pursuit of lavender success. "It's not so much about a state of being as it is an attitude. Until a few years ago, I would have to describe myself as being out of the closet with a chip on my shoulder." She continued, "For most of my life, I was out, but not open to other people. And by that I mean that I thought I had to do it all myself, because no one would want to help an ambitious lesbian reach the top of her field—and that was an attitude that nearly cost me my career."

In her drive to be successful, Janis not only had to bear the entire burden of achieving her dreams, but also alienated nearly all of her colleagues along the way. "I came up really fast and gained a whiz-kid reputation. For whatever reason, I just have a sixth sense about art." Janis developed a very impressive track record well before she turned thirty, which, according to her, "pissed a lot of people off." It was an attitude that she cultivated and embraced. "For a long time I actually relished having other people in my profession despise me. I even took pride in it! I told myself it was because they were jealous of my success, and that being collegial would have no impact on my career." Janis found out that even if you're exceptionally talented in your field, it's impossible to sustain success when you're cut off from colleagues and peers.

"I'm nothing if not practical," she said. "I was forced into the realization that the reputation I'd earned wasn't just as a whiz kid. Finding out there's no one in your field that will work with you, let alone hire you for your next job, was sobering. I knew that if I didn't do a fast attitude adjustment, it would mean my professional death." This sobering realization occurred at a professional luncheon where, quite by accident, Janis overheard a conversation about herself. "The worst thing about overhearing people talk about you is that since they don't know you're there, it's going to be brutally honest." What she had called the "chip on her shoulder" had isolated her from just about everyone in her field. "My first reaction, of course, was to see red. I thought, 'How dare they say these things about me? They're just a bunch of losers, and I don't need them anyway.'" About a week later, Janis was having dinner with her sister, and she told her what had happened. "I expected her to agree with me, that the opinions of these people were irrelevant to my professional life. But what I got was more like a cold bucket of water poured over my head. In one breath, she told me that I was nasty, self-consumed, and insecure and had brought all of this on myself. This time I didn't see red. I started to cry."

Over the course of the next year, Janis entered therapy and accepted that it wasn't her talent isolating her in a "jealous world," but her own fear of rejection. I asked her about the role her sexual orientation played in her "get them before they get me" attitude. "There were a lot of reasons, going back to my childhood, which contributed to my pushing people away. One of them was that I was overweight. Also right up there at the top of my list was an awareness at an early age that I was attracted to other females. And I knew that wasn't acceptable to a whole lot of people. Even though I had supportive parents and grew up in a fairly liberal area, I still felt the reality of being someone who wasn't 'suitable' or 'presentable' to the world at large." She continued, "You can't help but feel that way when you have so many angry, hateful people getting air time to condemn you. Hearing someone talk about AIDS being a blessing from God because it kills all of the right people leaves an indelible impression on you when you're just starting to figure out who you are." Janis eloquently summed up her own career difficulties. "That's where my 'get them before they get me' behavior was rooted. My reaction wasn't to hide or go into the closet. My modus operandi was to beat everybody else up before they could beat me up. I never recognized there was a huge penalty to pay for that behavior. You can't succeed in life by hating, even under the guise of professional brilliance. It led me down a lonely and difficult path."

In the last two years, Janis has spent a lot of time mending fences in her professional life. She told me, "It's much harder to get people to look at you with fresh eyes when there's a negative history surrounding you, but I'm doing it. Some people may never give me a chance, and that's something I have to accept. But I'm amazed at how some people I thought would never give me another chance have actually become my friends. Work isn't a fight anymore, and it feels wonderful. In fact, life isn't a fight anymore, and that feels even better."

Transforming Your Goals into Achievements

Most of us prefer to see results sooner rather than later, whether we're trying to lose weight, lower our blood pressure, or pay off bills. When we're investing our time and energy, we want to reach our goals as quickly as possible. Let me be the first to tell you that there's nothing wrong with wanting results as quickly as possible. In fact, the sooner you begin to take action on your road to success, the sooner you'll realize all of your professional dreams. But if you attempt to go from zero to sixty in your career "as quickly as possible," there's a chance you might skip over an important part of the career development process. And, as we've already discussed, starting in the middle leads to a wide variety of professional difficulties. But here's the good news: you've already done the work through the exercises in this book, and you're ready to take action.

EXERCISE **Taking Action**

You already have all you need to succeed—you have yourself and your dreams. Your lavender road to success puts you in charge of your own professional future. It's time to put together your answers from selected exercises throughout the book in order to create a road map that's tailor-made just for you.

1. Acknowledge that your unique identity is the source of your success.

   Using your answers to the exercises titled "It All Starts with You," "Integrating Your Abilities to Maximize Your Success," and "Your Image Matters" in chapter 9, complete the chart below to highlight all of the attributes represented by your unique identity.

   I can succeed and be free to pursue my dreams in the world of work because my unique identity holds these tremendous values.

MY INDIVIDUALITY	MY TALENTS	MY SKILLS	MY EGO

2. Identify where you want your road to take you.

   Based on your work in the exercises titled "Describing the Professional Benefits of Workplace Freedom" in chapter 3 and "Becoming the Author of Your Success Story" in chapter 6, make a list of your career goals and objectives. Also, feel free to incorporate any new insight or direction you've discovered that may now become part of your professional future. Remember that your dreams are valuable because they're your dreams. You have the ability to make each one of them an achievable reality.

3. Identify potential employers where you can succeed as yourself.

   List five organizations you believe can provide you with the opportunity to realize your career goals. The "Resources" section in the back of the book will lead you to specialized information about the policies, culture, and values of various organizations. Pay close attention to the alignment between your own interests, abilities, and values and those of an organization.

4. Determine if the workplace realities of your identified employers are worthy of your time, talent, and dedication.

   Now, using your answers from the exercises in chapter 9 titled "Are There Other Gay People Here?" "Knowing What It Takes to Get Recognized," and "Being Proud of What You Do," identity the realities of the workplace environment offered by your five potential employers. Write a brief summary of each organization's internal reality, success factors, and external image. Then rank your list of five employers. Identify, in order, which workplace environments are most aligned with your unique identity.

5. Explore appropriate opportunities with optimism, empowerment, and professionalism.

   List three specific steps you can take to explore opportunities with the organizations you've identified. Examples of steps you might take include:

   - Asking for an information interview
   - Investigating an organization through their website
   - Researching a company through online resources like www.hooversonline.com or www.vault.com
   - Reading an annual report
   - Joining a professional association
   - Networking with other gay people in your fields of interest

Making "Lavender Success" Your Success

There is absolutely no doubt in my mind that, as a community, we are strong and influential. We have the ability, both collectively and individually, to succeed beyond our greatest expectations. In a perfect world, no human being would ever be prevented from pursuing his or her career dreams. Yet as we know, this isn't a perfect world. It's far from it. However, accepting less than you deserve in your professional life isn't something you have to live with in this imperfect world.

Overcoming prejudice and bigotry doesn't require their extinction, although wiping out ignorance and hate should always be our ultimate goal. You can overcome prejudice and bigotry and therefore the negative influences of homophobia in your professional life starting now. Ask yourself if you can stay where you are and be successful. Achieving your dreams in your current location is possible if it affords you the opportunity to be valued as a human being. If instead you're in a place where anti-gay sentiments abound, success may be waiting for you in a brand-new professional home.

Wherever you are sitting at this very moment, believe in the wisdom that each person in this book has shared with you, and accept the strength of their amazing experiences. Know that you have everything you need to be successful. Believe in the value of your unique identity and your dreams will come true. Hold your head high and move forward into your future. Enjoy your lavender road to success.

National Organizations

American Civil Liberties Union (ACLU)

www.aclu.org

The ACLU is dedicated to keeping America safe and free for all people. You will find a great deal of information for the gay community, including up-to-date information about issues related to discrimination, domestic partnerships, civil unions, gay marriage, and transgender rights.

Equality Project

www.equalityproject.org

The Equality Project monitors the policies dealing with sexual orientation at major corporations, and presses companies to implement progressive policies. You will also find information on this site about shareholder activism for the gay community.

Family Pride Coalition

www.familypride.org

The Family Pride Coalition supports and protects families with gay, lesbian, bisexual, and transgender parents. You will find information about events and groups as well as a library of specialized publications and articles.

Gay and Lesbian Victory Fund

www.victoryfund.org

The Gay and Lesbian Victory Fund is the leading national political organization that recruits, trains, and supports open lesbian, gay, bisexual, and transgender candidates and officials. You will find valuable information about current political races and issues across the country.

Gay Financial Network

www.gfn.com

The motto of the Gay Financial Network is "Your Money. Our Lives. It's Time." In addition to valuable information about everything financial, from retirement plans to home loans, you'll also find a career section with job listings. There are examples of resumes along with interview tips.

Gay, Lesbian, and Straight Education Network (GLSEN)

www.glsen.org

GLSEN works to create safe schools for lesbian, gay, bisexual, and transgender people. There is a lot of information at this site for people in the field of education as well as information related to fighting to end antigay bias in K–12 schools.

Gaywork.com

www.gaywork.com

In partnership with monster.com, this site provides job listings with gay-friendly organizations as well as company profiles and other employment resources.

Gender Education and Advocacy (GEA)

www.gender.org

GEA is a national organization focused on the needs, issues, and concerns of gender variant people. Their website provides information and resources that educate and advocate for anyone who faces gender-based oppression.

Human Rights Campaign WorkNet (HRC)

www.hrc.org/worknet

Working for lesbian, gay, bisexual, and transgender rights, the HRC provides resources and information related to a wide variety of issues for members of the community in the world of work. The HRC corporate equality index and the annual "State of the Workplace" publication provide invaluable information about the internal realities of various organizations.

International Gay and Lesbian Human Rights Commission

www.iglhrc.org

The mission of the International Gay and Lesbian Human Rights Commission (IGLHRC) is to secure the full enjoyment of the human rights of all people and communities subject to discrimination or abuse on the basis of sexual orientation or expression, gender identity or expression, and/or HIV status. If you're considering going to work in another country, you will find important information to help you make informed decisions.

Lambda Legal

www.lambdalegal.org

Lambda Legal is a national organization committed to achieving full recognition of the civil rights of lesbians, gay men, bisexuals, transgenders, and people with HIV or AIDS through impact litigation, education, and public policy work. On this site you will find state-by-state laws addressing antidiscrimination and domestic partnerships.

National Center for Lesbian Rights (NCLR)

www.nclrights.org

NCLR is a progressive, feminist, multicultural legal center devoted to advancing the rights and safety of lesbians and their families. Their site provides information about various projects and events around the country as well as online publications.

National Gay and Lesbian Task Force (NGLTF)

www.ngltf.org

The NGLTF leads national efforts to coordinate legislative activities and grassroots organizing nationwide on a variety of issues important to gay, lesbian, bisexual, and transgender people. Through this site, you will find information about issues ranging from civil rights and education to hate crimes and HIV/AIDS. A calendar highlights events taking place around the country.

Out & Equal Workplace Advocates

www.outandequal.org

Out & Equal provides support and advocacy to the lesbian, gay, bisexual, and transgender community in the workplace. Each year the organization's Workplace Summit provides a national forum directed toward educating human resource professionals and developing LGBT Employee Resource Group (ERG) leadership.

Parents, Families and Friends of Lesbians and Gays (PFLAG)

www.pflag.org

PFLAG is an organization comprised of parents, families, and friends of lesbian, gay, bisexual, and transgender persons that celebrates diversity and envision a society that embraces everyone, including those of diverse sexual orientations and gender identities. Their website offers a great deal of educational information as well as links to chapters and resources that educate and advocate for the community.

Professional Associations

Federal Globe

www.fedglobe.org

This site lists information and contacts for gay, lesbian, bisexual, and transgender employees of the federal government.

Gay and Lesbian Medical Association (GLMA)

www.glma.org

GLMA exists to make the health care environment a place of empathy, justice, and equity. The site provides information for LGBT physicians, medical students, and other health care professionals, as well as millions of LGBT patients throughout North America who seek equality in health care access and delivery.

National Consortium of LGBT Resources in Higher Education

www.lgbtcampus.org

The consortium's mission is to achieve higher education environments in which lesbian, gay, bisexual, and transgender students, faculty, staff, administrators, and alumni have equity in every respect. You'll find a variety of information and resources on this site specific to the field of higher education, including job listings.

The National Lesbian & Gay Journalists Association (NLGJA)

www.nlgja.org

The NLGJA is an organization of journalists, online media professionals, and students interested in the journalism industry whose goal is to foster fair and accurate coverage of lesbian, gay, bisexual, and transgender issues. The NLGJA actively opposes workplace bias against all minorities and provides professional development for its members.

National Organization of Gay and Lesbian Scientists and Technical Professionals (NOGLSTP)

www.noglstp.org

This is a national organization of gay, lesbian, bisexual, and transgender people (and their advocates) employed or interested in scientific or high-technology fields. NOGLSTP's goals include dialogue with professional organizations, disseminating information, and improving professional environments for its members.

Pride At Work

www.prideatwork.org

The newest constituency group of the AFL-CIO (American Federation of Labor & Congress of Industrial Organizations), Pride At Work mobilizes mutual support between the organized labor movement and the gay community around organizing for social and economic justice.

Regional Organizations

Albuquerque Lesbian & Gay Chamber of Commerce (ALGCC)

www.dssw.com/algcc

The ALGCC acts as the primary resource for the gay, lesbian, bisexual, and transgender business community.

Bay Area Career Women (BACW)

www.bacw.org

BACW is an organization where women who love women come to network, socialize, and give back to the community. The organization also has a business fund that supports lesbian projects and services within the San Francisco Bay Area lesbian community.

Business Alliance of Los Angeles (BALA)

www.balaweb.org

BALA is a group of gay, lesbian, and gay-friendly businesses, professionals, and individuals who have joined to promote business networking for its members and the community at large in Los Angeles's San Fernando Valley.

Colorado Business Council (CBC)

www.coloradobusinesscouncil.com

The CBC is a statewide equal-opportunity chamber of commerce comprised of gay and gay-supportive business owners and professionals.

Desert Business Association (DBA)

www.dbaps.com

The DBA is the largest specialized chamber of commerce serving the gay, lesbian, bisexual, and transgender community in the greater Palm Springs, California, area.

East Bay Business and Professional Alliance

www.lavenderchamber.org

The East Bay Business and Professional Alliance is an organization of lesbian, gay, bisexual, and transgender business owners, professionals, and community leaders. The alliance promotes and serves its members and acts as a community-building, networking, and business development resource for the GLBT San Francisco area–East Bay community.

Golden Gate Business Association (GGBC)

www.ggbc.com

The Golden Gate Business Association began as the nation's first business organization founded by gay and lesbian entrepreneurs. For more than twenty-eight years GGBA has been a dynamic and active voice for the San Francisco Bay Area's professional community.

Greater Boston Business Council (GBBC)

www.gbbc.org

The GBBC's mission is to foster and promote the vitality and productivity of the gay, lesbian, bisexual, and transgender business and professional communities in the greater Boston, Massachusetts, area. The council seeks to promote a positive image of GLBT citizens and to strengthen their position in society by providing opportunities for the personal, professional, and social growth of its members. There is a focus on networking with other GLBT professional organizations, both locally and nationally.

Greater Phoenix Gay and Lesbian Chamber of Commerce (GPGLCC)

www.gpglcc.org

The mission of GPGLCC is to build the strength and prosperity of the gay and gay-friendly community in Phoenix, Arizona, through networking and social activities. Founded in 1980, GPGLCC has become part of the nation's largest and most progressive gay, lesbian, and gay-friendly organizations in the United States, representing a wide range of professions and fields.

Greater San Diego Business Association (GSDBA)

www.gsdba.org

GSDBA is "San Diego's Lesbian and Gay Chamber of Commerce," a nonprofit organization dedicated to building strength and prosperity in the lesbian and gay community through networking and social activities.

Greater Seattle Business Association (GSBA)

www.the-gsba.org

GSBA's mission is to expand opportunities for the lesbian, gay, bisexual, transgender, and allied community in Seattle, Washington. The organization advocates for the exchange of ideas, increased visibility, and promotion of inclusiveness in the workplace and also sponsors scholarships.

Inland Northwest Business Alliance (INBA)

www.inbaspokane.org

INBA is a nonprofit organization of gay and gay-friendly businesses, professionals, and individuals who have joined together to create a safe and comfortable atmosphere for individuals to network and socialize in Spokane, Washington.

Las Vegas LAMBDA

www.lambdalv.com

LAMBDA is a nonprofit business organization for gay business owners, professionals, entrepreneurs, and the community at large in Las Vegas, Nevada. Its goal is to provide an environment of success for the lesbian, gay, bisexual, and transgender community through the exchange of ideas, information, and resources.

Long Beach Community Business Network (LBCBN)

www.lbcbn.org

Founded in 1992 by gay and lesbian business owners, LBCBN serves as a networking and support organization for gay-owned and gay-friendly businesses within the greater Long Beach, California, area. LBCBN assists members in marketing and promoting their businesses as well as helps new businesses establish themselves in the area.

Network of Business and Professional Organizations (NBPO)

www.nbpo.org

In New York City, NBPO is organized to foster communication and cooperation among the area's diverse lesbian and gay professional organizations. The organization holds networking and social events, with the participation of several independent member groups, to raise funds for worthwhile nonprofit lesbian and gay social service organizations. NBPO also sponsors educational forums and panels on subjects of interest to the community.

OutFront Minnesota

www.outfront.org

OutFront Minnesota's mission is to make their state a place where GLBT Minnesotans have the freedom, power, and confidence to make the best choices for their own lives.

Portland Area Business Association (PABA)
www.paba.com

PABA is an organization in Portland, Oregon, made up of businesses and individual professionals interested in business and networking. The organization exists to promote business and offer support to its membership, which is made up of gays, lesbians, and gay-friendly friends and associates.

Potomac Executive Network
www.pendc.org

PEN is a nonprofit, nonpartisan, all-volunteer network of more than 1,000 gay, lesbian, bisexual, and transgender professionals who work for business, nonprofits, or government in Washington, D.C., Virginia, and Maryland. PEN works to build bridges across D.C.'s GLBT community, bringing together men and women of all ages and backgrounds to form a dynamic network that helps each person succeed.

Selected Research Websites

Hoovers Online: The Business Information Authority
www.hooversonline.com

Hoovers Online offers a free level of access to information about specific companies, including their financials. You can also search for people holding key jobs in various companies as well as view recent news articles. For a fee, you can subscribe to a secondary level that will give you a more in-depth profile.

PR Newswire
www.prnewsire.com

On this site you can access breaking news from tens of thousands of organizations around the globe. It's a good resource to find out what type of information exists relative to specific employers.

Salary.com
www.salary.com

On this site you can enter job titles along with your zip code and view salary ranges in your current field or a field you are exploring.

Salary Expert
www.salaryexpert.com

This is another site that allows you to enter job titles and zip codes to find out what you can expect to get paid.

Vault
www.vault.com

This is another resource with both free and paid levels of access. You can find out what a day in the life is like with respect to different jobs and in various organizations. There is also a job board as well as information about law and MBA schools.